Lost Restaurants of GALVESTON'S AFRICAN AMERICAN COMMUNITY

Lost Restaurants of GALVESTON'S AFRICAN AMERICAN COMMUNITY

INTRODUCTION BY
W. DWAYNE JONES

GALVESTON HISTORICAL FOUNDATION
WITH GREG SAMFORD, TOMMIE BOUDREAUX, ALICE GATSON AND ELLA LEWIS

AMERICAN PALATE

Published by American Palate
A Division of The History Press
Charleston, SC
www.historypress.com

Front cover, clockwise from top left: courtesy Rosenberg Library; courtesy Oliver family; courtesy Rosenberg Library, Galveston, Texas; courtesy Rosenberg Library, Galveston, Texas; courtesy Rosenberg Library, Galveston, Texas; Galveston Historical Foundation.
Back cover: courtesy Rosenberg Library, Galveston, Texas; *top inset*: courtesy of Cornelia Harris-Banks; *bottom inset*: courtesy Watkins family.

Unless otherwise noted, all images are courtesy of the Galveston Historical Foundation.

First published 2021

Manufactured in the United States

ISBN 9781467141772

Library of Congress Control Number: 2021934121

Notice: The information in this book is true and complete to the best of our knowledge. It is offered without guarantee on the part of the authors or The History Press. The authors and The History Press disclaim all liability in connection with the use of this book.

Dedicated to the memory of Galveston's African American chefs, restaurant owners and their support staff, who, through their combined efforts, set high standards that ensured customer satisfaction and a lifetime of cherished memories still shared today.

Contents

Acknowledgements

The authors would like to extend their sincere appreciation to the following people for their time spent granting requests for interviews and, in many cases, for their donations of photographs included in the book. A few of these kind and patient souls have passed away since the project to document the lost restaurants of Galveston's African American community began. Those who helped along the way include Vander Caldwell-Haynes, Jay Carnes, Tommie Davis, Gloria Ellisor, Curtis Lee Gillins, Sharon Gillins, Cornelia Harris-Banks, Denise Harrison, Diane Henderson, Jimmy Lee Hilton Sr. (deceased), Lettie Holden, Galveston County commissioner Stephen Holmes, Joyce Ann Hunter-Daniel, Steve Jack, Vanessa Jefferson, Vesterie Johnson-Merchant, Nathan Kennie, Debra James Liedy, Lillie Little, Ransom Lundy, Tommie McNeil, Mary Milburn, Herman Mills (deceased), Madeline Mills (deceased), Ward Nesbitt, Marion Oliver III (deceased), Marion Oliver Jr. (deceased), David O'Neal Jr., Clora Otems, Larry Parson, Odessa Phillips, Avys Poe, Sherrod Poe, Anthony Priestly, Roger Quiroga, Joe Rendon, Sarae "Toni" Rex, Georgia Robbins, Ned Rose, Margaret D. Scurry, Maggie Shabazz, Lucy Smith Taylor, Reverend Jerry Temple, Leonce Thierry Jr., Lawrence Thomas, Alice Thompson, Lena Thompson, Reverend Kerry W. Tillmon, Ann Walton, Rosalind Wilkins, Melvin Williams (deceased) and Gilbert Zamora Jr. Special appreciation is also extended to the staff at Gaido's Seafood Restaurant as well as to Lauren Martino, Kevin Kinney and Sean McConnell at the Galveston and Texas History Center located at Galveston's Rosenberg Library.

Introduction

Food and foodways are a cherished part of every ethnic and cultural group. Celebrating food, whether in real time or virtually, undergirds our human spirit and strengthens ties between family and friends. This publication is the work of our dedicated African American Heritage Committee at Galveston Historical Foundation. It meets monthly to identify opportunities for educating and sharing the history of African Americans on Galveston Island and work to preserve the legacy of our historic Rosewood Cemetery.

From decades of enslavement to modern concepts of freedom, Galveston's African American story is fascinating. African American men and women served as inspirational educators, church leaders and pillars of our community to make up the great story of Galveston. The stories are often unheard voices of the past and, when collected, offer a beautiful glimpse into that past. This publication captures a few of those stories that left an imprint on a special genre of local food history.

Without detracting from this work, it is interesting to connect the food here with the development of an important annual event in Texas and now the United States. Juneteenth (June 19) commemorates the reading of General Order Number 3 on that day in 1865 in Galveston. At the close of the Civil War and with the surrender at Appomattox in April 1865, Union forces distributed themselves across the Confederate states to end armed combat and inform the enslaved of their freedom. Stemming from President Abraham Lincoln's reading of the Emancipation Proclamation

The city of Galveston in 1894, looking northeast toward the business district. By 1900, the city's port was a national leader in cotton exports.

Looking southeast toward the Gulf of Mexico in 1894, at residential wards known today as the neighborhoods of San Jacinto, Kempner Park and Old Central.

The Osterman Building (*left foreground*), where General Order Number 3 was released on June 19, 1865. The order, issued by U.S. general Gordon Granger, ended slavery in Texas.

on January 1, 1863, these declarations in 1865 carried the message as well as immediate direction to the enslaved. Major General Gordon Granger's release of General Order Number 3 proved to be one of the last official notices of the war. It also signaled the presence of federal troops, the end of conflict and the control of a different government.

In January 1866, African Americans in Galveston held a sizeable demonstration on the anniversary of Lincoln's proclamation that in the course of time moved to the June 19 date of General Granger's announcement in Texas. From appellations such as "Emancipation Day" to the eventual name, "Juneteenth," more than 150 years passed until contemporary discussions of the event brought international attention to the date and its significance. The annual celebration in many communities and its recognition as an official holiday by Texas and some local governments makes Juneteenth a significant day for African Americans and others as well. This event today is rarely celebrated without reminders of its significance and associated foodways in the community.

While Juneteenth is a most remarkable day each year, Galveston's African American history is full of accomplishment: Norris Wright

Juneteenth is celebrated nationwide. A historic marker on the Strand at Twenty-Second Street was dedicated in 2015 and marks the site where the Osterman building once stood.

Cuney's political and labor leadership, early exemplary education for African Americans still noted in the Old Central Community Center, the independence of establishing a separate cemetery at Rosewood for those excluded from other cemeteries, the sports achievements of Jack Johnson and the work of Jesse McGuire Dent to gain equal pay in Texas for African American teachers and educators. It is unlikely that any social or civil rights advancement occurred without a strong association of local food traditions and many of the locally owned food-related businesses.

Galveston is truly honored to have a long and invaluable African American history that continues to be uncovered and told. This small segment of the local history is written here to continue that narrative. You will want to read this work and share it among your friends and family. It is the only place that recounts good eats and good eating places from our African American heritage on the island, many that linger in the minds of Galvestonians, past and present.

Chapter 1

Restaurateurs and Chefs

ANDREW AUGUSTUS "GUS" ALLEN

There will always be historians who will discuss the many individuals who have made significant contributions to the rich history that surrounds Galveston Island, and the name Gus Allen should always be mentioned in those conversations. Andrew Augustus "Gus" Allen Sr. was born on May 24, 1905, in Leesville, Louisiana, the grandson of slaves. He arrived in Galveston in 1922 and would rise to become the owner of Gus Allen Enterprises and one of Galveston's best-known African American entrepreneurs. The term *entrepreneur* is used frequently to describe Allen. His business interests were as diverse as the city he lovingly referred to as home. Allen always told family, friends and employees that "success comes before work in the dictionary." He used the phrase quite frequently and always made sure he put in the hard work. During his long tenure as a successful businessman, Allen built motels, barbecue pit stops, restaurants, coffee shops, clubs and apartment buildings, all catering to African American patrons. In a July 25, 1980 edition of the *Forward Times Metro Weekender*, Allen took little credit for his success and instead praised the people he met along his business journey, whose advice he recognized gave him the knowledge he needed to succeed. Without those people, Allen acknowledged, the success he experienced might not have happened.

When Allen arrived in Galveston in 1922, he found work at the historic Hotel Galvez on Galveston's Seawall. He shined shoes in the hotel lobby and

Gus Allen (*center frame*), with friends. *Courtesy Rosenberg Library, Galveston, Texas.*

was responsible for keeping the lobby clean. Seeking better job opportunities, Allen soon moved to Houston. Jobs in Houston weren't much better, so Allen relocated again, to Kansas City, and became part of the "Great Migration." Six million African Americans sought to escape racial segregation and discriminatory laws in the rural South and moved to the urban areas in the North and West between 1916 and 1970.

From Kansas City, Allen moved to Chicago and then Detroit before he landed in the Big Apple. New York was not for him, however, and soon he was on the move again. He headed back down south and ended up in Biloxi, Mississippi, where he met a couple who owned an upscale restaurant close to the Gulf of Mexico. They offered Allen a job as a waiter in the dining room, which he was also responsible for cleaning. Around the same time, Allen met E.C. Noey, who operated the local train station in Biloxi. Allen's son Donald stated that Noey assisted his dad in the development of the management and leadership skills he became known for later in life. While in Biloxi, Allen's son Andrew Augustus Jr. was born in 1926. As a new father, Allen took the opportunity to begin to save money and would put aside a few dollars every payday. By 1930, he had saved over $300; he used the money to return to Galveston, where he wasted no time building his legacy.

Gus Allen's Café, located at Twenty-Eighth Street and Seawall Boulevard. *Courtesy Rosenberg Library, Galveston, Texas.*

Gus Allen (*seated, left*) with son Gus Allen Jr. and secretary Marie Pines.

In Galveston, Allen's uncle William owned a boardinghouse and café at 2704 Church Street. He leased the building to Allen, who later said he put on his apron and immediately opened the Dreamland Café. Allen hit the ground running and sold chili for ten cents a bowl and two pork chops for a quarter. A steak dinner cost forty cents; a fish sandwich would only set you back a dime. If you couldn't make it down to the Dreamland to get your supper, Allen delivered. One evening, a gentleman came into the café and ordered a fish sandwich. Staff regretfully informed him that they had sold out of fish. The customer, who had previously partaken of a few adult beverages, said in a jocular tone, "fry some shrimp, I'll eat them." To Allen's knowledge, that had never been done in the past, as he had only seen shrimp boiled and served in cocktails with red sauce. Allen battered up the shrimp, dropped them in the fryer and produced what is believed to be the first known fried shrimp sandwich on the island.

By the middle of the 1930s, Allen changed the name of the Dreamland Café to Gus Allen's Café. Allen was now looking for ways to expand. Armed with the wisdom to invest in property and the ability to set aside a little of his profit in order to purchase real estate when it became available, Allen acquired the building next door to the café in 1937 and opened a boardinghouse when America was in the middle of the Great Depression. The Depression hit African American citizens the hardest, and Allen was there to step up and assist those who were suffering.

As America entered the 1940s, World War II became a reality. Gus Allen Jr. joined the U.S. Navy. On the homefront, the café continued to serve the citizens of Galveston. In 1947, an industrial accident occurred at the Port of Texas City, known as the Texas City Disaster. The explosion killed 581, injured over 5,000 and destroyed or damaged over five hundred buildings that left 2,000 people homeless. People from Galveston County and across the state and the nation stepped up to assist those in need. Allen contributed by organizing fundraisers and arranging lodging for the celebrities who came to lend their support, including musician Louis Armstrong and actor Eddie Anderson, known as "Rochester" on *The Jack Benny Show*.

Allen's efforts to expand his business enterprises always focused on creating businesses where African Americans felt welcome. In 1947, he leased a building to Nelson "Honey" Brown and played a significant role in launching Brown's culinary career. Brown opened Honey's Barbecue in the leased building and served legendary barbecue to the citizens of Galveston for four decades. A few months after Honey's opened, Allen opened the Gus Allen Hotel at 2711 Church Street as well as a barbershop next door at

The former Dreamland Café, owned by Allen, located at 2704 Church Street.

2709 Church. With his hand already in the barbecue game, thanks to Honey Brown, Allen pivoted and turned his attention to seafood. His good friend Albert Fease had culinary aspirations with seafood and wild game. Allen was certain that Fease would be successful as a restaurateur, so he backed his friend when Fease opened Fease's Café, later known as the Jambalaya Café, in one of Allen's buildings. According to Allen and confirmed by his son Danny, Fease introduced stuffed shrimp to local seafood menus when he filled a butterflied shrimp with fresh crabmeat, dipped it in batter and dropped it in the fryer. As the years passed, Fease perfected his stuffed shrimp recipe and even added variations to his menu.

As the 1940s rolled into the 1950s, Allen's business moves helped define African American life in Galveston for the next three decades. In 1952, the Gus Allen Café went through a transitional period that led to Allen turning the business over to John S. Temple. He and his wife took control of the daily operations and eventually changed the name to Temple's Café. Around the same time, Gus Allen Jr. opened a café at 2818 Avenue R ½ and named the business Little Gus Allen's. Located on the same block as Albert Fease's business, all of the 2800 block of Avenue R ½ would soon belong to Allen. The block was located on the Seawall and directly across the street from the segregated beach opened to African Americans. After Allen purchased the block on Seawall, he acquired several buildings along the 2700 block of

Interior of Gus Allen's Café, located at 2828 Avenue R ½. *Courtesy Rosenberg Library, Galveston, Texas.*

Church Street, where he opened the Savoy Beauty Salon in 1952. It was located directly across the street from the Gus Allen Hotel and barbershop. Allen eventually leased the beauty shop to Laura M. O'Neal, who took over management of the business.

By the late 1950s, Little Gus Allen's Café had closed and a new business was preparing to open at that location close to the Seawall. According to Danny Allen, his dad began to consider retirement. Allen had accumulated a lot of property by that point and could have lived comfortably without working. Instead, Allen continued to work and added another challenge to his daily roster when he joined the civil rights movement in an effort to ensure that the African American citizens of Galveston as well as African American visitors to the island had places to shop, lodge and find entertainment. In 1960, Kelton D. Sams Jr., a junior at Galveston's historic African American Central High School, rallied several of his classmates and led the first "sit-in" lunch counter demonstration at the local Woolworth's on Market Street. Arrangements were made between religious, civic and business leaders, and in April 1960, the lunch counters of Galveston were integrated. During that time, Allen yielded to no one in his eagerness to share his desire that all traces of Jim Crow laws, customs and attitudes be eradicated. He continued to make every effort to provide a place on Seawall Boulevard for African Americans. In 1965, Allen opened the Gus Allen Villa and Café in the 2800 block of R ½. One year after he opened the restaurant and villa, Allen purchased the building next door and demolished it to make way for a new building he erected that added fifteen rooms to the villa. When it was completed, Allen relocated the café to the first floor of the new building, and the café's old space, located on the corner of Twenty-Ninth and R ½, was remodeled and opened as a coffee shop and lounge.

Tragedy struck the Allen family several times over the next decade. Andrew Augustus "Baby Gus" Allen III was killed in action on February 25, 1968, in Vietnam while serving with the United States Army. Andrew Augustus Allen Jr. passed away on January 26, 1971. Around the same time, through eminent domain, some of Allen's real estate holdings north of Broadway were seized by the City of Galveston. It was a point of contention that troubled Allen. He felt that the African American community predominantly located on that side of Broadway was being treated unfairly, so he began to advocate for single-member districts within Galveston's city government. The change occurred and paved the way for Allen's son Danny to be elected to serve District 2 on the city council in 1993, a position he held until 2000.

In 1972, Allen and his wife, Bertha, were honored by Prairie View A&M University as Parents of the Year after they were nominated by Danny during his junior year at the university. Shortly after, Allen made the decision to close the Gus Allen Hotel at 2711 Church Street in order to focus his attention on the Seawall location. Bertha Allen retired from day-to-day responsibilities at the Villa on the Seawall in 1977. She had been a significant part of the success of Gus Allen enterprises for more than fifty years. She passed away on January 2, 1981. Born in Beaumont, Texas, in 1906, Bertha had moved to Galveston in 1923.

Andrew Augustus "Gus" Allen passed away on June 16, 1988. His service was held at Galveston's Holy Rosary Catholic Church, the oldest African American Catholic church in the state of Texas, followed by interment at Galveston's Memorial Cemetery. He was survived by four daughters, Darlene Allen Scott, Diane Allen Cole, Daniela Allen McIntosh and Debbie Allen Scott, and two sons, Danny and Donald.

During his life, Gus Allen always considered every possibility when he approached a decision. As a result, he enjoyed success at multiple levels. Longtime friend Vic Fertitta still praises his friend's "solid business mind and talent, limited by segregation." Civil rights icon Dorothy Height once said,

"Greatness is not measured by what a man or woman accomplishes, but by the opposition he or she has overcome to reach his goals." Andrew Augustus Allen Sr. overcame a wealth of opposition and achieved a level of greatness in life that stands as a model to all of humankind.

RECIPES

The following recipes are from Gus Allen's ledger books, held within the archive at the Galveston and Texas History Center at Rosenberg Library, Galveston, Texas. Recipes are transcribed as written in the books.

Honey Battered Fried Chicken

1 chicken
3 tablespoons honey
4 tablespoons milk or cream

Beat honey and cream well. Salt and pepper chicken. Roll lightly in flour. Dip in honey batter and roll in flour again. Drop in hot grease. Turn often. When done, mop with melted butter

Sauce [sounds like barbecue sauce but just noted as "sauce" in the ledger books!]

½ bottle of ketchup
1 tablespoon barbe-q spice
2 tablespoons Worchester sauce
1 tablespoon red pepper
1 tablespoon onion salt
½ teaspoon garlic salt
1 tablespoon chili powder
½ cup vinegar
½ cup water

Cook. Add 1 tablespoon butter at end

White Cake

Materials
1 cup oleo or butter
2½ cups sugar
1–1⅛ cups egg whites
1½ teaspoons almond extract
4½ cups cake flour
2¼ teaspoons baking powder
1 cup milk

Procedure
A. Cream butter and sugar together in a mixer.
B. Add egg whites, beat thoroughly in mixer—add almond extract.
C. Sift flour and baking powder and add alternately with milk—do not beat.
D. Pour batter in loaf or pound cake pans.
E. Bake at 300 to 325 degrees for 45 minutes to 1 hour.
F. For layer and sheet pans bake at 350 to 375 degrees from 20 to 25 minutes.

Lemon Filling for Cakes

½ cup sugar and ¼ cup flour: Mix in top of double boiler. Stir in—
1 cup warm water
3 well-beaten egg yolks

Cook and stir over hot water until thick. Cover. Cook 5 minutes more and add:
2 tablespoons grated lemon peel
Juice of 1 lemon
2 tablespoons butter

Mix. Cool. Fills 1 two-layer cake.

ALBERT FEASE

Albert Fease was born in Lafayette, Louisiana, on March 8, 1911, and arrived in Galveston in the late 1920s. In the early 1950s, Fease opened the Albert Fease Café at 2820 Avenue R ½. A short time later, the business moved to 2812 R ½, where it remained. After relocating, the establishment was renamed Jambalaya Beer. In 1955, the name of the business changed again, to Jambalaya Café. Fease remained the proprietor for the duration of the business. Through his association with the café and community events, Fease left an indelible mark on the history of Galveston Island.

Fease's Jambalaya Café was known for its famous stuffed shrimp, stuffed flounder and gumbo, as well as jambalaya. In addition to seafood, the restaurant also served steaks and other short-order dinners. Fease would bring back wild game he shot on hunting trips to the café, where he served it to lucky customers. One patron, Ransom Lundy, remembers that everything on the menu was exceptional and served in generous portions. Lundy especially loved the shrimp jambalaya.

Fease's café was also equipped for banquets and private parties. The *Galveston Daily News* recognized the restaurant in 1955 for its donation to the United Fund of Galveston. Longtime Galveston educator L.A. Morgan was honored at the Jambalaya on October 20, 1963. The news also reported that the Jambalaya hosted a dinner for the Central High School Quarterback Club on November 11, 1966. The café also hosted the annual Holy Rosary father-son breakfast that continues to this day. The *Galveston Daily News* reported that on May 19, 1968, Galveston Independent School District superintendent Morgan Evans spoke at the Jambalaya Café about the upcoming integration of Galveston Ball High School at the start of the 1968–69 school year.

According to lifelong Galveston resident David O'Neal, Central High School student athletes would make the long drive back to Galveston to eat after an athletic event, specifically so they could dine at the Jambalaya. The road games would often take them to Beaumont, Baytown and Houston. Those destinations had great restaurants, O'Neal remembered, but the players would hold their appetite until they returned to Galveston and Fease's Jambalaya Café.

In addition to operating the café, Albert Fease was an avid sportsman. He enjoyed golfing, fishing and hunting and won many awards participating in tournaments supporting his interests. Multiple mentions in the *Galveston Daily News* reported on Fease's victories in both local and regional tournaments.

Top: A table of patrons celebrates at Albert Fease's Café, located at Seawall Boulevard and Avenue R ½. *Courtesy of Cornelia Harris-Banks.*

Bottom: A 1968 Galveston City Directory advertisement for Albert Fease's Jambalaya Café.

In the January 16, 1969 edition of the newspaper, sportswriter Jimmy Blair interviewed Albert Fease on the recent victory by Charles Sifford at the Los Angeles Open. Fease was a huge fan of Sifford, who was the first African American to play on the PGA tour in 1969 and was the first African American inducted into the World Golf Hall of Fame in 2004. Sifford's first attempt to qualify for a PGA tour failed at the 1952 Phoenix Open, where he played by invitation obtained through former world heavyweight champion Joe Louis Barrow. Fease was quoted in the 1969 article as saying, "It does

Fease's Café interior. The café was located across the street from the segregated beachfront where African Americans were allowed to gather. *Courtesy of Cornelia Harris-Banks.*

prove that you're never too old to hit it 'big' once in a lifetime." Fease praised Sifford as a good sportsman and a fine golfer, and he always mentioned Sifford's love for cigars. A few years later, Fease and Sifford played in a tournament together in Miami, Florida, and in 2014, Sifford was awarded the Presidential Medal of Freedom by President Barack Obama.

In addition to operating the café and participating in sporting events, Albert Fease also served as a board member for the reorganization of the Gibson branch of the YMCA and was a member of the Knights of Pythias Dokos, the Galveston Isle Golf Association and the Golftoppers Outdoor Sportsman's Club. Fease attended Holy Rosary Catholic Church, the first African American Catholic church in the state of Texas.

In addition to running the café and participating in sporting events, Fease also operated the Sinclair service station at 2902 Seawall Boulevard, just one block west of the café. The facility was a "full service" station, offering supreme gasoline, supreme motor oil and kerosene, as well as washing, polishing, lubrication and tire and battery services. The station rewarded its customers with Plaid trading stamps.

Albert Fease passed away at St. Mary's Hospital in Galveston on September 25, 1981. He had been a resident of Galveston for fifty-two years

Fease's restaurant was a popular spot for both the local African American community as well as tourists visiting the area. *Courtesy of Cornelia Harris-Banks.*

and a restaurant owner for thirty-three years. He was survived by his wife, Margie Lee Fease, daughter Linda Faye Beasley, eight sisters and numerous nieces and nephews.

The funeral service for Albert Fease was held at Holy Rosary Catholic Church under the direction of Fields Funeral Home. He was interred at Galveston Municipal Cemetery. Members of the Texas Peace Officers Association and the Knights of Pythias Dokos served as honorary pallbearers.

Fease was a well-rounded ambassador for the city of Galveston. He left a legacy that is still held in the highest regard by those whose paths he was able to cross. His substantial contribution to the rich history of Galveston Island will never be forgotten.

THOMAS DEBOY "T.D." ARMSTRONG

Thomas Deboy Armstrong was born in Meeker, Louisiana, on November 11, 1907, to Thomas and Mary Armstrong. Thomas was the only boy of eight children. The family lived on a sugarcane plantation, but when

Thomas was six years old, the family moved to Port Arthur, Texas. After he graduated from high school there, Thomas attended Tuskegee University in Alabama before he transferred back to Texas to attend Prairie View A&M College, where he graduated in 1929. He returned to Port Arthur and taught six years at Lincoln High School, where he had graduated from high school. While teaching, Thomas married Marguerite Gertrude Goodwin of Beaumont, Texas. To this union, daughter Thelma Dolores was born in 1935, followed by son Thomas II, born in 1950.

Thomas resigned from teaching and worked two years on a boat operated by the United States Office of Coast Survey before he moved his family to Galveston in 1938. On the island, Thomas found employment as an assistant manager of Strode Funeral Home. Over the years, T.D., as he was known around town, became a very successful businessman who owned several properties, businesses and companies employing numerous Galvestonians. His ownership included T.D. Armstrong Real Estate, Tyler Life of Texas Insurance, T.D. Armstrong Investments, as well as apartment buildings, a barbershop, a beauty shop, a Laundromat and a service station. When he purchased the Strode Funeral Home and became owner, he changed the name to Strode Armstrong Mortuary. On Thirty-First Street, T.D. owned the Shamrock Motel, the little Shamrock Motel Junior and Armstrong's Drug Store.

Armstrong's food-service businesses were the Shamrock Café, the adjoining restaurant to the Shamrock Motel, and the Fountain, located inside Armstrong's Drug Store. Vesterie Johnson-Merchant was hired as a waitress at the Shamrock Café the summer of her sophomore year of college in 1962. She worked during the days that summer, but when classes resumed that school year, she worked at the café only on weekends. She recalled the restaurant being open twenty-four hours and customers being offered a variety of entrées, sides, desserts and beverages. She could not remember the average cost of a meal, but she did recall making great tips—as much as $125 a week during the summer!

When you ask African Americans who were teenagers or young adults in the 1940s, '50s and '60s if they remember T.D. Armstrong's Drug Store, they always say with a smile, "Yes, I remember that drugstore!" The Fountain inside the store was very popular. The drugstore was located on the corner of Thirty-First and Avenue L, a few blocks from Central High School and the football stadium. It was the place to go after school, for after-school events, football games and on weekends. There was a jukebox, and Armstrong always made sure it was stocked with the latest and most popular

Right: Thomas Deboy "T.D."Armstrong (1907–1972), named one of "America's 100 Richest Negroes" by *Ebony magazine* in May 1962.

Below: Armstrong at his office in Port Arthur, Texas. Date unknown. *University of North Texas Libraries, The Portal to Texas History, Museum of Gulf Coast.*

tunes. Five cents was all it cost to play your favorite song. The food was great, too, as Tommie Davis remembered. A hamburger and fries could be purchased for thirty-five cents; a soft drink was ten or fifteen cents. The chili and spaghetti was Ned Rose's favorite. A variety of sandwiches, hot dogs, chili dogs, chili, ice cream, shakes and malts were also served. Everyone's favorite beverage was the cherry Coke. Nathan Kennie recalled hanging out with friends outside the drugstore at night. Well-known African American police officer Leroy "Buster" Landrum monitored the area and removed the congregated crowds by saying, "Give me the corner!"

Kennie's father and Officer Landrum were good friends, so Kennie was always able to go back into the drugstore to wait for his then girlfriend, who worked there, to finish her shift. When she was a high school student, Joyce Ann Hunter-Daniel had to get permission to go to any of her school's night events, and her younger brother had to go with her. After basketball games and other events, Daniel remembered, her brother walked with her and her friends to Armstrong's Drug Store so she could get her favorite drink—the famous cherry Coke. After she enjoyed the drink, she and her brother caught the bus and went home. Vander Caldwell-Haynes, now ninety-four years old, recalled purchasing hamburgers and drinks and added enthusiastically that "T.D. Armstrong's Drug Store was the place to hang out!" While they both attended Central High School, Herman Mills and Madeline Roche never met. One day, when Herman was visiting Armstrong's, it was love at first sight when he saw Madeline working the soda fountain. She said she was not interested in him. He recalled, "But she sure made really good hamburgers!" They eventually became friends; after a long courtship, the two married on July 17, 1965.

Armstrong's was also the place to keep the community informed of upcoming events. The drugstore sold tickets to local football games, concerts and boxing matches and was always willing to advertise any community event. Above the drugstore, a large lounge was available to rent, where the public or community organizations could host teas, receptions, parties and other functions.

T.D. Armstrong was very active in the community and supported the YMCA, the Boy Scouts of America, the Boys Club and several other nonprofit organizations. He was a member of the board of regents of Texas Southern University and the board of trustees of Wiley College. He also served on several boards in Galveston and across the state and nation. He was an active member of the Democratic Party and was selected twice to attend the Democratic National Convention as the community's representative. In

The Fountain Luncheonette at Armstrong's Drug Store, located on the corner of Thirty-First Street and Avenue L. *Courtesy Rosenberg Library, Galveston, Texas.*

Interior of Armstrong's Drug Store, from an advertisement placed in a Central High School yearbook. *Courtesy Old Central Cultural Center.*

The Little Shamrock Hotel and Shamrock Café were located in the same block as Armstrong's Drug Store. *Courtesy Rosenberg Library, Galveston, Texas.*

1961, T.D. became the first African American elected to Galveston's city council since Norris Wright Cuney was elected a city alderman in 1883.

His personal wealth was noted in printed articles in *Ebony* magazine and other publications. In September 1961, *Ebony* included a story about T.D., "Negro Politician Makes Good in Texas—Plantation-Born Ex-Teacher Rises to Wealth and Post on Galveston City Council," followed by an article in the

May 1962 issue that declared T.D. one of "America's 100 Richest Negroes." The list also included Harry Belafonte, Nat King Cole, Johnny Mathis and Floyd Patterson. T.D. Armstrong passed on December 28, 1972, at age sixty-five. Most, if not all, of his property has been destroyed, demolished or sold, but his legacy lives on through the memories of everyone who was lucky enough to know him.

CLARY MILBURN

Clary Milburn was born on October 10, 1940, in Opelousas, Louisiana, and attended schools within the Opelousas school district. The son of sharecroppers, Milburn experienced firsthand a life of hard work. His dad, Rodney Dale Milburn, worked as a self-employed carpenter; his mother, Mary L. Milburn, was a homemaker. Milburn inherited a strong work ethic from his parents and, in turn, passed it on to the next generation of the Milburn family.

In 1957, Milburn left Louisiana and moved to Galveston. The first job he acquired on the island was with the maintenance department at John Sealy Hospital at the University of Texas Medical Branch (UTMB). He later worked at John Sealy's Hospitality Shop, the hospital's restaurant. There, his coworkers waited patiently to have Milburn fix their sandwiches at lunch. In the hospitality shop, Milburn met his future wife, Galveston native Doris Winters. When she passed away in 2012, the couple had been married for fifty-two years.

After his initial introduction to the food-service industry at the hospitality shop, Milburn later brought his strong work ethic to Gaido's Seafood Restaurant and eventually to the Pelican Club, a private members-only dining area within the historic restaurant. It was an era when the Pelican Club was known as much for its customer service as for its delicious seafood. In that environment, Milburn excelled. He was often described as the "best of the best" of an elite group of waiters selected to work the club. While he worked for the Gaido family, Milburn also worked part time as a cook at the Jack Tar Hotel, once located across from Stewart Beach. While he maintained those two jobs, he also launched his own janitorial business, which eventually grew to serve more than 150 clients. While Milburn worked tirelessly, his daughter Angela Milburn-Thomas commended her mother for her own determination and drive to improve. Doris and Clary put their children's needs first and foremost. Once the kids were older, Doris enrolled in Galveston College's medical administration program. After she graduated, she worked as a unit clerk at UTMB before transferring to the accounts payable department, where she was responsible for the campus janitorial department and, later, for the university's restaurant, where she had met Clary so many years earlier.

In 1977, Milburn opened Clary's Seafood Restaurant. With encouragement from business partner Harry Fiegel and several loyal customers, Milburn combined his experience and exceptional culinary knowledge to embark on a business adventure that would grow to legendary status. The kitchen was completed first, allowing Milburn to operate as a catering service to the many businesses located on Port Industrial (Harborside) Boulevard. This created a customer base that was ready-made when the restaurant opened its doors for business later that year. Located at 8509 Teichman Road, the restaurant had a unique location, not in proximity to the seawall, where tourists flocked. Instead, it was located off the beaten path, quietly situated on Offatts Bayou and close to the Galveston Causeway, where customers in the know could easily drop by on the way in or out of town. The location also made it easy for mainlanders to hop onto the island for an excellent meal followed by a quick trip back home when they were finished.

Milburn's younger brother Jimmie said that Milburn learned a lot about cooking after he moved to Galveston but noted that he had a good foundation built from countless family meals served up back in Louisiana. There, Milburn learned how to add that Cajun flair and flavor to the seafood he served. Jimmie remembered his personal favorite was the flame-broiled shrimp that he and his coworkers at a nearby automobile dealership often ordered during their lunch breaks. Milburn's sister Alice Perry worked at the restaurant for over fifteen years. During that time, she left her mark on the dinners and the diners. Alice took genuine pride in her brother's restaurant and prepared everything from scratch. She never stopped looking for ways to improve the quality of the food they served. If something needed to be done, if someone had to step up, Alice was always willing to put in the extra effort to maintain the high quality of food expected by their loyal customers.

Seth Sharpe became a waiter at Clary's when it opened in 1977. Over time, his role evolved into manager of catering before he became the official maître d' for the restaurant. Sharpe spent close to twenty years working at Clary's and has very fond memories of the time he spent there. He recalled a menu that offered a variety of Louisiana-style seafood, including gumbo,

The south side of Clary's Seafood Restaurant, 8509 Teichman Road, overlooked Offatts Bayou.

shrimp, oysters and fish cooked a variety of ways. The general consensus was that everything was delicious, but it was the service and ambience that customers remembered. Milburn exemplified southern hospitality, and that brought back his loyal followers just as much as did the exquisite food. His ability to remember returning guests and their previous menu selections made for an interesting discussion when one entered his restaurant, as Milburn put as much effort into his interpersonal communication skills as the chefs did crafting meals in the kitchen. Kathy Munoz, former news director at KLST-TV in San Angelo, Texas, recalls the first time she and her family visited Clary's. They arrived a little after closing time, but Milburn invited them inside to eat anyway. His warm hospitality made such an impression on the Munoz family that they stopped by Clary's Restaurant to eat every time they came to the island. A great conversation starter when one entered the restaurant was the photographs of Milburn's celebrity patrons decorating the restaurant walls. The celebrity tributes began when Milburn's brother Rod won a gold medal at the 1972 Summer Olympic Games and his stepson Charles Alexander Jr. led Galveston Ball High to the 1975 Texas University Interscholastic League AAAA Track & Field Championship. Alexander was eventually drafted by the Cincinnati Bengals and participated in Super Bowl XVI in 1982. Whenever he got hungry for some great Cajun seafood, Alexander made the trip to Galveston accompanied by his two daughters. Alexander later perfected C'Mon Man Cajun Seasoning and credited Milburn and stepbrother Dexter with helping him perfect the sauce marketed throughout Texas and Louisiana.

Milburn and Doris were the parents of seven children, many of whom worked in the family restaurant. Son Dwayne started working for his dad at age six and learned the foundation of his father's service principles at an early age. Dwayne worked in every capacity imaginable at the restaurant, starting as a busboy before becoming a barback, then bartender and finally bar manager. As manager of the restaurant bar, Dwayne crafted and promoted special cocktails that complemented items on the menu. He noted that the grilled oysters were the most popular menu item and recalled how many seafood restaurants in the area added them to their menus after their staff had experienced the dish for themselves at Clary's. When asked about his favorite dinner they served, without hesitation, Dwayne named the seasoned baked shrimp, which had a smoky flavor that made for an unforgettable dish. Dexter Milburn started cooking for his father's restaurant during his sophomore year at Ball High School. Dexter credited his father with teaching him valuable lessons that keep him in demand as a chef to this day. He has fond memories of the "Leonville Creole" dish that was very popular at the restaurant and at every private event the restaurant catered. The dish included bell peppers, onion, shrimp, sausage and seasoned beef served over rice. The recipe came from Milburn's mother, and Dexter praised his Aunt Alice, who always prepared the dish to perfection. Dexter noted that staff always looked for ideas to make the meals more appealing and was always improving the menu selections. When the kitchen introduced its southern-style green beans to the menu, they quickly became a crowd favorite. From 1979 to 1992, Milburn's third son, Wayne, served as the manager. With food and drink covered by his sons, Milburn's daughters Angela Thomas and Rosetta Cooper managed the restaurant office. The siblings have fond memories of working together.

Michael Hypolite worked at Clary's for over thirty-five years and served most of that time as the kitchen manager. He fondly remembers the "Saralyn B" platter as his favorite dinner at the restaurant and recalled with delight the buttered crab, baked shrimp, grilled oysters and baked fish that made up the platter. He is quick to mention that nothing but fresh crabmeat was used to stuff the flounder. The buttered crab, also a favorite dish, took a lot of effort to prepare. He also recalls the preparation required for the popular grilled oysters that were prepared on ceramic plates. The extreme heat required to grill the oysters caused the ceramic plates to crack, which became a challenge to overcome. One day, Milburn walked into the kitchen and presented Hypolite and Chef Dexter Milburn with a stack of metal muffin pans and offered them as the solution to the cracked ceramics. Grilling the oysters in the pans solved the problem and kept the dishwashers busy—on a normal Friday or Saturday evening, the muffin pans would go through repeated cleanings in order to keep up with demand. The restaurant's seafood-eggplant dressing was also a favorite among Milburn's customers. The eggplant was mixed with shrimp, crabmeat and a secret seasoning, making it one of the restaurant's most popular side dishes. The dish was originally offered only at catered and private events, but Milburn occasionally offered it to his restaurant patrons, and it became so popular that he added it as a permanent menu item.

Former Galveston city manager Douglas Matthews grew up in the same neighborhood as Milburn's wife, Doris, and began a friendship with Milburn that grew to a level of mutual respect. Matthews described Milburn as personable, classy and always a gentleman and noted that those are compliments that have to be earned. Matthews believed Milburn earned them by the example he set. The Matthews family looked forward to eating out at Clary's Restaurant on a weekly basis. While he compliments every selection on the menu, Matthews's favorites included anything with lump crabmeat, the shrimp dinners and the grilled red snapper. Like anyone else who ate there, Matthews mentioned how Milburn came and greeted everyone during their visit. It was a rare quality that separated Milburn from others and ultimately was the contributing factor in patrons' return visits for a guaranteed fine-dining experience.

Robert E. Dowdy Sr., retired senior pastor at the Church of the Living God in Galveston, met Milburn in 1982 through a mutual friend. After the Milburn family began attending evening services at Dowdy's church, the two men became fast friends. Reverend Dowdy and his wife became regular customers at Clary's Restaurant, and after each meal, Milburn pulled up a chair and had lengthy discussions with the couple. Milburn and Mrs. Dowdy discussed recipes while he and the reverend discussed spiritual issues. Dowdy loved the restaurant's shrimp "All-Seasons" dish and remembered Milburn sharing the seasoning blend he used on the shrimp. When Milburn learned that he and Mrs. Dowdy's mother shared the same birthday, he insisted they have dinner every year in the restaurant together, with birthday cake for dessert. Every summer, when the youth from Dowdy's church attended camp, Milburn insisted on helping to provide meals for the students. Dowdy and Milburn built a strong bond over the years, and to this date in his pastoral study, Reverend Dowdy has a photograph of his friend Clary Milburn on his wall.

In early September 2008, Milburn had an uneasy feeling about an approaching hurricane in the Gulf of Mexico named Ike. He had his daughter Rosetta go to the restaurant and pick up important papers and

Clary Milburn (1940–2016) inside his restaurant. *Courtesy Milburn family.*

documents. At her dad's request, she made her way to the restaurant that September morning and removed all of the company's important documents. That proved to be a wise decision, as the restaurant's location on Offatts Bayou was later identified as ground zero for the storm's high water level. No one could have predicted the kind of damage it inflicted on the restaurant, with over six feet of floodwater inside the beloved establishment. It was a long recovery for the restaurant and the staff, but after a year of hard work, the restaurant reopened. By 2015, Milburn's health started to fade and he was forced to spend less time at the restaurant. His absence was reflected in the decline in the number of patrons, and family members made the difficult decision to close the business that December. On January 31, 2016, Clary Milburn passed away surrounded by his loving family. Reverend Dowdy officiated at the funeral service, held at Moody Memorial Methodist Church, followed by burial at Forest Park East Cemetery in Webster, Texas.

The life of Clary Milburn will live on in the lives of those who were fortunate enough to spend time with him. There is no better example of that than the life of his grandson Justin Milburn, who fondly remembers his grandfather taking him horseback riding and spending time with him. Milburn's daughter Charlotte Mays credits her dad with teaching her about leadership, accountability and determination to find your passion, work hard and never give up on your ability to succeed. Rosetta Cooper treasures her memories of time spent with family and friends working in the restaurant and recalls meeting Jack Nicholson and Shirley MacLaine while they filmed scenes in the restaurant's dining room for the 1996 movie *Evening Star*.

It is difficult to find a superlative to describe the life of Clary Milburn that would honor him properly. He had the extremely rare ability to transcend race, political ideology, gender and social class. Humorist and author Will Rogers once said, "You must judge a man's greatness by how much he will be missed." The man, Clary Milburn, and his restaurant, Clary's, passed into eternity in proximity. Although the man and the establishment are greatly missed, Clary Milburn is remembered as the standard for what is great in humanity.

Clary's Seafood Eggplant Casserole
Shared by Rosetta Milburn Cooper

Clary's easy baked Seafood Eggplant Casserole is delicious even if you are not a fan of eggplant. Clary served the dish at his restaurant and most of the private events he catered. It stands alone as a main entrée or as a side dish.

Prep/cook time: 1 hour, 15 minutes
(oven, 30 minutes at 350 degrees Fahrenheit)

Ingredients:
3 tablespoons butter
1 medium onion
3 garlic cloves
8 cups eggplant, peeled and cubed
½ cup water
1 teaspoon salt
½ teaspoon black pepper
1 teaspoon dry parsley
3 green onions, chopped
1 ½ cups bread crumbs

2 cans cream of mushroom soup
1 cup milk
2 cups, 16 ounces, fresh lump crabmeat

Topping:
½ stick butter, melted
1 cup bread crumbs
1 cup grated cheddar cheese

Melt butter over medium heat in large saucepan. Sauté onions and garlic 6 minutes, then add cubes of eggplant with water. Cook about 15 minutes; will decrease in size. Remove from heat, add salt, pepper, parsley and bread crumbs. Last but not least, add lump crabmeat. In a separate bowl, add cream of mushroom soup and milk. Stir mixture until smooth. Pour into eggplant mixture, stir and put into casserole pan. In a separate bowl, stir bread crumbs with melted butter and grated cheese and spread on top of mixture.
Bake at 350 degrees Fahrenheit for approximately 30 minutes
Serves 8.

WADE A. WATKINS

A native Texan from Leon County, Wade A. Watkins was born on February 6, 1925, in Oakwood. When he was ten years old, his mother died, and his aunt Addie Edwards took him into her home and raised him as her own son. In 1948, after he served in the U.S. Army and worked in the food-service industry in San Antonio, Watkins came east to Galveston, where he met and married Elisa Broussard. His first job on the island was as a cook at the Buccaneer Hotel on Galveston's famed Seawall Boulevard. Knowing that he might be laid off during the off-season, Watkins joined the kitchen staff at the historic Gaido's Seafood Restaurant, established in 1911. Watkins not only survived that first winter but also became an indispensable part of Gaido's kitchen and was soon named the restaurant's executive chef.

Chef Wade Watkins proudly displays his diploma from LaVarenne Cocking School in Paris, France. *Courtesy Watkins family*.

Watkins was a quiet, generous, soft-spoken man of God. He attended the prestigious LaVarenne Cooking School in Paris, France, was a longtime member of the Texas Chefs Association and was honored with several other culinary awards. He was respectful and polite to everyone he met. He was held in the highest esteem by his peers as well as by the Gaido family. His career as Gaido's chef spanned three generations of the Gaido clan. With an imposing physical stature, massive hands, good looks and an easy laugh, Watkins was a natural leader. Through that leadership and by the example he set, Gaido's kitchen still reflects Watkins's performance and work ethic. Affectionately and respectfully known throughout his career as "Big Daddy," his influence endures through his recipes. Gaido's menu still features dishes named after Watkins, like its famous Watkins' Shrimp Bisque and the special way of cooking fish "Wade Style," prepared with a dusting of specially seasoned flour and finished with lemon.

After forty-four years of service at Gaido's, Watkins retired in 1993. His daughter Mary Milburn credits her mother, Elisa, and Mike Gaido for her father's successful career as a chef. In 2013, Watkins died at the age of eighty-eight. During his lifetime, he and his wife resided in La Marque,

Watkins *(far right)* poses with the staff of LaVarenne Cooking School in Paris, France. *Courtesy Watkins family.*

Gaido's Seafood Restaurant in 1967, where both Watkins and Clary Milburn worked during their careers. *Courtesy of Gaido's Seafood Restaurant.*

Texas. He was a faithful member of Shiloh AME Church in Galveston for sixty-five years and sang in the men's choir, was a member of the church's board of stewards and cooked on more than one occasion for the entire congregation. Watkins was also a member of the Masonic Grand Lodge. In 1998, he and Elisa were honored for their service in their neighborhood, where they cared for their handicapped neighbors and provided food and clothing to the local nursing home. So, the next time you are in Galveston, stop by Gaido's Restaurant and remember to ask to be seated in the Wade Watkins Dining Room.

Wade Watkins's Signature Bisque

2 pounds onions, diced
Vegetable oil
5 tablespoons margarine
1 cup water
1 ½ pounds tomatoes, chopped
½ pound carrots, diced
4 cups heavy cream
2 ½ ounces lobster base
¾ teaspoon cayenne pepper
¾ teaspoon white pepper
Kitchen Bouquet to taste

In a large saucepan, sweat the onions in a little vegetable oil over medium heat for 20 minutes or until cooked through. Add margarine, water, tomatoes and carrots and cook until the vegetables are tender, about 30 minutes. Place the mixture in a food processor or blender and process to a smooth puree. Press though a fine mesh strainer and add to a large, clean saucepan. Discard solids left in the strainer. Add cream, lobster base, cayenne pepper, white pepper and Kitchen Bouquet. Bring mixture to a boil, stirring constantly. Simmer 25 minutes or until reduced to 6 cups. Strain before serving. Top with 2 ounces of cooked shrimp, lobster or crab per serving.

Chapter 2

Diners, Grills and Inns

THE SQUEEZE INN

In 1948, Mary Richardson and her husband, Steve, bought a small house that served as the family's principal dwelling upstairs and provided space for a tiny, aptly named, family-operated eatery downstairs. As far as places to eat went, the Squeeze Inn restaurant was off the beaten path—so far off, in fact, that it was located in an alley in the 3900 block of Winnie Street. However, despite the location, the place was filled to capacity each day at lunch as city officials, attorneys and average, everyday working people stopped in for a homestyle meal with taste appeal at a very affordable price.

When the restaurant first opened, Richardson and her husband mostly sold barbecue dinners with all of the fixings to the occasional group of customers who stopped in. After Steve's death, Mary needed to expand the menu to appeal to a larger group. Her daughter Carrie Jack joined her in the day-to-day operation of the business that was serving as an eatery by day and a juke joint by night. When the Squeeze Inn closed after lunch, Carrie Jack worked a full-time job on the night shift at UTMB.

The two had a simple standard for running the restaurant: fresh food cooked daily, nothing served from a can and leftovers never served. The menu changed every day, but a sample lunch selection consisted of crispy fried chicken, barbecue ribs, fried fish, crab cakes or meatloaf. Side dishes were rice and gravy, potato salad, mustard greens, black-eyed peas, cabbage, corn and baked macaroni. Every meal was accompanied by their famous homemade rolls.

The Squeeze Inn Café, located on the alley at Thirty-Ninth and Winnie Streets. The café contained very few tables, so many patrons got their food "to go." *Courtesy of Rosenberg Library.*

With only six tables for dine-in customers, the Squeeze Inn filled up quickly every day at lunch. Most patrons ordered their meals in take-out containers to go. An old-fashioned cash register rang up the satisfying lunch that sold for less than five dollars with a steady clatter while the jukebox offered up the soulful sounds of the popular artists of the day.

News of the restaurant, its location and its reputation of great taste on a budget spread quickly among community members who had never been to that part of town. Doug Mathews, the first African American city manager in Texas, recalled how city administrators and secretaries in their finest business attire quickly exited City Hall at lunchtime and raced in their expensive cars to the Squeeze Inn, where they lined up in the alley and waited for the renowned fried fish and crab cakes.

Richardson and Annie Mae Charles, a well-known figure in the Galveston community, were lifelong best friends. Because of this friendship, Charles used her association with prominent Galveston professionals and paid visits to attorneys and lawmakers to introduce the soulful foods served at the Squeeze Inn. As a result of her efforts, they became frequent customers. Marvin Zindler, a well-known anchorman for Channel 13 KTRK News in Houston, did a feature story on the restaurant and included the report in a news exposé on the best soul food restaurants in the Houston-Galveston area.

After she became ill in 1992, Richardson closed the beloved restaurant she had run for forty-six years. She died in 2000, and most of the memorabilia from the Squeeze Inn was destroyed in Hurricane Ike. Her grandson Steve Jack currently resides in the tiny structure, squeezed in a little spot in an alley that was once known as the "Best Soul Food Served in the County."

THE HAVENETTE DINER

The Havenette Diner was a soul food diner located at 902 Twenty-Ninth Street, across from the Cedar Terrace housing units. There, one could find such meals as pork chops, pork steaks, fried chicken, chitlins, rice, beans, cornbread and mustard greens, to name a few. In 1968, Leon, known as "Neat," and Marie James took over ownership from his sister Mary Helen Hall, who also owned and operated the Havenette Beauty Salon.

The diner was open Monday through Saturday from 5:30 a.m. until about 4:45 p.m. Neat and Marie always made sure they were there early in order to be able to catch the crew who worked on the wharf and were always looking for a hot cup of coffee and a homemade breakfast. Neat usually had to leave for his regular job before the breakfast rush was over. As breakfast service was going on, plans for the noon meal were underway, and once breakfast was over, lunch was already cooking. If someone came in between meals, Marie whipped up something especially for them; she never wanted to see anyone go hungry.

Every day, when it came time for lunch, calls were already being received at the Havenette Beauty Salon, located next door to the diner, asking what Marie was cooking and what that day's dessert was. Orders for lunches were often placed as early as 10:30 a.m. in order to ensure the special of the day was still available when the caller came around to claim their meal an hour later. When Marie's daily special was revealed, it was the first thing to sell out. Every patron claimed that Marie really did make the best homemade pies in the city. Thursday was known as "chitlin day," and preparations for that meal always started on Wednesday before the diner closed. The Jameses' daughters always said that cooking chitlins would never be on their list of things to do—to do them right simply required too much work!

Neat worked his regular job at Century Papers Company but always stopped by the diner to see how things were going and to lend a hand if needed. Neat and Marie, along with their children, were indeed a working family team. They never met a stranger, and every customer was like a member of their family. The young people who lived in Cedar Terrace stopped by in the mornings before they went to school to purchase the infamous moon cookies for their lunches or to eat on their way to school. Some of them even stopped by in the afternoon to get help from the daughters with their schoolwork. It was a fun and enjoyable time to get to know the neighborhood kids and become a part of their lives.

Marie loved her customers and always gave back to them by hosting an annual Thanksgiving appreciation meal. The meal was free and was her way of showing her customers how thankful she was for their patronage. Her customers were just as thankful and always bestowed monetary gifts upon her every holiday season, as they truly appreciated all she did for the community. In September 1986, the Havenette Diner closed after the passing of Neat and Marie's eldest son, Leon "Billy" James. A few months later, Marie suffered a major stroke. Neat and their other children, Phil, Teresa and Debra, helped with her care until she passed away in November 2003. Daughter Teresa James-Ivory passed away in 2006. Neat still lives in Galveston and still enjoys life. The James family will always be grateful for all of their extended Galveston family who came to the diner to eat or to share a good meal and good conversation with good friends.

The Twilight Grill

Maggie Fisher, better known as Big Momma, was born and raised in Marshall, Texas, and moved to Galveston many years later. She and her daughter Mary Fisher Scurry and son John Fisher Jr. quickly fell in love with the island city and decided to make it their home. Maggie acquired a large property; the family lived on one side of the house, and the other side became an establishment known as the Twilight Grill.

Located at the corner of Thirty-Fourth and Winnie, the Twilight Grill quickly became a local favorite for hearty midday meals, especially among the men who worked on the Galveston wharves and surrounding cotton sheds. Big Momma's soul food menu of basic, down-home cooking was just the thing needed to sustain them through a laborious day's work. Big Momma did not disappoint. Her typical lunch menu consisted of mouthwatering pork bones, pork chops, crispy fried chicken and scrumptious meatloaf. Side dishes were usually rice and gravy and a choice of red beans, butter beans, black-eyed peas, tangy cabbage or mustard greens. Homemade cornbread and yeast rolls laden with butter accompanied each meal, and the mandatory Kool-Aid was always available. On Fridays and on special days, the menu included cornmeal-battered fried fish fresh from the Gulf of Mexico. No meal was complete without a slice of her delicious pound cake topped with jelly icing. Every Friday, Big Momma personally delivered lunch to her son-in-law at his job at the Light Company, which, coincidentally, was also his payday! On Saturdays, patrons enjoyed a lighter fare of hot dogs, chips and drinks, as Big Momma only opened for the working lunch crowd during the week. Six of the upstairs rooms doubled as a rooming house. The tenants' evening meal each day at six o'clock came from leftovers from the lunch menu offered earlier in the day.

Twilight Grill owner Maggie Fisher (1903–1980). *Courtesy Fisher family.*

The Twilight Grill was also a center for entertainment at night and on weekends and often featured a Zydeco band. Loyal patrons could run a tab to purchase beer, wine and sodas, ensuring a good time would be had by all. Whenever Big Momma got word that the Texas Rangers were in town, pinball machines used for entertainment magically disappeared upstairs!

Despite the heavy workload she managed with the help of her daughter, Big Momma never missed two things: keeping her beauty shop appointment each week and going to church on Sunday. When her health failed, Maggie Fisher decided to close down her beloved Twilight Grill, and the building was later demolished. Though the building is no longer there, memories of down-home soul-food meals, seasoned with Big Momma's love, remain.

THE UNION GRILL

In the middle of the 1930s, during the Great Depression, two different Galveston businessmen opened establishments in separate locations that catered to Galveston's African American community. They started a journey that would be passed on to others with similar business interests and ended at a single location: 2826 Avenue R ½. At that location, Jesse Modicue opened the Virginia Pavilion sometime between 1934 and 1935. Modicue was born in Marshall, Texas, in 1897. At about the same time, Frank Ford opened the Union Grill at 2527 Postoffice Street. Ford was born on August 14, 1892, in Bay City, Texas. In addition to managing the Union Grill, Ford worked as a dockworker and was a member of the International Longshoremen's Association (ILA) Local 329.

Over the next few years, both Modicue and Ford operated their establishments that served the citizens within their different neighborhoods. In 1938, Allen Nichols took over management of the Virginia Pavilion and changed the name to Union Grill #2. By 1939, the Union Grill was still operated by Frank Ford, but Leonard Jackson assumed ownership of Union Grill #2. In the early 1940s, David Fanuiel took over operations at #2, and by 1943, he had passed the baton to James Brown. Management of Union Grill #2 would change again a few years later.

It is not known of the connection between the owners of the two locations. Union Grill #2 surpassed the original location by close to ten years. It started during the Great Depression and operated on a block that would help define the African American community on the Galveston Seawall Boulevard.

Frank Ford died on March 20, 1941. He is interred at Municipal Cemetery in Galveston. Jesse Modicue passed away on September 10, 1954, and was buried at Memorial Cemetery in Galveston. In the late 1930s, Jesse's wife, Alma, operated the Red Dot Café at 2812 R ½. The café remained open for a little over a year before it closed in 1940.

UPTOWN TAVERN

L.C. "Stringbean" Gillins was born on April 12, 1926, the third child of ten and first son of Limos Chester Gillins and Annie Hollingsworth Gillins. According to his son Curtis Lee Gillins, "L.C." was his father's legal name and resulted when L.C.'s mother refused to name him Limos Chester, so only

Above: 2824 Church Street, where Up Town Tavern once thrived.

Left: L.C. "Stringbean" Gillins (1926–2007), proprietor of the Up Town Tavern. *Courtesy Gillins family*.

the initials were entered on his birth certificate. A family of sharecroppers, the Gillinses lived in Doylene, Louisiana, a village in the metropolis of Shreveport–Bossier City. L.C. moved to Galveston when he was in his early twenties and first found employment working at the grain elevator on the wharf as a longshoreman. His Galveston friends soon nicknamed him "Stringbean" because he was very thin and six feet, two inches tall.

L.C. was not the first child of Limos and Annie to move to Galveston. Curtis recalled being told that his Aunt Alma, the oldest child, hitchhiked to Galveston when she was in her mid-twenties. At that time, African Americans were seeking a better life and migrating to California and other states. Alma knew people who had moved to Galveston and found good jobs, so she made plans to join them. Curtis recalled family stories of Aunt Alma riding boxcars and hitching rides in order to make it all the way to Galveston. Alma had always been tough, he said, wearing overalls and a big cowboy hat and carrying a large switchblade knife. Within a few years of Alma's arrival in Galveston, all of the children moved to Galveston; eventually, the children moved their parents to Galveston, too. Their parents were still sharecropping, and the kids knew that the landowner seldom paid their parents fair wages and often told their father his sacks didn't weigh enough to pay the rent where they lived. Curtis was always told the children moved their parents in the middle of the night to avoid a confrontation with the landowner.

Marjorie Lewis was born and raised in Galveston, born to parents Albert and Rosa Lewis on March 21, 1926. L.C. and Marjorie met in the early 1940s at a USO dance in Galveston and were married on June 25, 1946. To their union, four children were born between 1947 and 1953: Annie, L.C. Jr., Curtis and Rodney.

When L.C. lived in Doylene, he worked in the fields with his family and was very impressed with those in his community who owned their own businesses. He often worked for a White man who owned a service station, and he admired an African American lady, Ms. Thigpen. She owned a "little hole in the wall" restaurant and sold barbecue and side dishes, like a bowl of red beans and rice for twenty-five cents. L.C. really wanted to own his own business. Annie, L.C.'s oldest child, recalled that her father, after he had worked regular jobs for over twenty years, borrowed money from his mother-in-law, Rosa Lewis, to lease a building at Twenty-Seventh and Church Streets. At that location, L.C. opened Little Harlem in the early 1950s. He didn't serve food, but he sold sodas, and even though he didn't have a license to do so, he also sold bootleg beer and liquor. Little Harlem had a jukebox and was just a place for people to socialize and have parties. There was a room in the back of the building for those who wanted to shoot craps or play cards. Curtis stated that his father kept order, quickly removing disorderly people and those who were getting too intoxicated. After several years, L.C. closed Little Harlem and purchased a large, two-story building at 2826 Church Street. He named the new business Up Town Tavern, but it was soon known by the community as Stringbean's.

Up Town Tavern was a full-service business. The first floor of the building was large enough to accommodate multiple dining tables, a dance floor and a stage where bands performed on Fridays and Saturdays. L.C. acquired a liquor license and sold beer, mixed drinks and sodas. Like Little Harlem, Up Town Tavern also had a jukebox and a back room for those who wanted to shoot craps and play cards. L.C. sold barbecue ribs, beef, links and chicken at Up Town Tavern as well as fish and boudin. Popular side orders were potato salad and beans. Up Town Tavern also occasionally sold wild game purchased in the neighboring communities of Wharton, Liberty, Dayton and El Campo. L.C. stored the wild game in a freezer at the restaurant and sold rabbits, squirrels and raccoons to anyone who wanted to take it home and cook it. He also sold boudin and deer sausage and would place a sign outside the building when wild game, boudin and deer sausage was available. Annie stated that these items sold well. He operated a lucrative business and even rented rooms on the second floor of the building.

Up Town Tavern closed after L.C. passed away on August 1, 2007. He was survived by eight children—four from his first marriage and four from his second and third unions: Essie, Kevin, Felicia and Beatrice. An effort to reopen the business after his death was diminished when Hurricane Ike caused extensive damage to the building.

KIMBROW'S LOUNGE

Louisiana native Frank "Kimbrow" Washington Jr. opened Kimbrow's Lounge in late 1975. Located on the corner of Winnie and Thirty-Seventh Streets, the establishment had two mailing addresses: 3701 Winnie and 703 Thirty-Seventh Street. Kimbrow's was a welcoming space in which one could sit and relax while enjoying an adult beverage. But Kimbrow's was also known for its "Soul Food" meals—a daily lunch special that included smothered steaks one day, pork chops another day. Oxtails also made the menu. The meal also included two side orders of vegetables, cornbread and a dessert. Wilson Matthews, a longtime employee of the University of Texas Medical Branch (UTMB), remembers getting meals from Kimbrow's in the 1970s and 1980s. He complimented the generous portions of food served with each meal. Michael D. Carnes worked nearby and recalled eating at Kimbrow's at least once a week. He mentioned that he believed he tried everything on the menu. Carnes fondly remembered the rice and gravy he ordered with every meal. He noted that the gravy was so good, you knew instantly it was homemade and not a mix that came out of a package. It was that extra care that brought you back to Kimbrow's again and again.

Kimbrow Washington passed away at his residence on June 28, 1994. He was survived by his wife of forty years, Irene, and daughters Elaine and Betty. His service was held at Holy Rosary Catholic Church under the direction of Carnes Brothers Funeral Home with the burial at Lakeview Cemetery in Galveston. Kimbrow's remained in business for a few short years after Washington passed away and served the same quality food and generous portions. In the late 1990s, the lounge shut its doors for good and brought to a close over twenty years of service to the citizens of Galveston. A final goodwill gesture by Washington was to ask that all donations be given to the Richard L. Haller Memorial Scholarship Fund at Holy Rosary Church. Deacon Haller was a teacher for many years in the Galveston Independent School District and retired from Weis Middle School in May 1980.

The building that once housed Kimbrow's Lounge is now home to Allen's Kitchen & Grill. The establishment opened in 2017 under the direction of proprietress Rita Allen. Her mother was Joyce Lee "Momma" Figgins Simpson of the Figgins barbecue family. Ms. Allen's father was Joseph Simpson Sr. of Simp's Kitchen. The Simpson children all learned how to cook from experienced family members who passed the legacy of Galveston's African American restaurateurs and chefs to the next generation. On most days when Allen's Kitchen is open, you will find Rodney Allen there helping his mother. His great-grandmother would be proud knowing the torch has been passed to the fourth generation.

SIDNEY'S DRIVE-INN

During the late 1950s and 1960s, the new idea of drive-in cafés became popular. A person could drive up to a diner, and staff would walk out or

Melvin Sidney and his staff in front of his drive-in restaurant. *Courtesy Rosenberg Library, Galveston, Texas.*

sometimes roller-skate to their car to take a food order. Staff returned with the food once it was prepared and encouraged patrons to remain in their cars with family and friends or take the food home. In Galveston, Melvin Sidney embraced this new dining concept.

Melvin Sidney was born in Cedar Lane, Texas, on October 14, 1918. He attended Galveston public schools and graduated from Central High School in 1936. He worked as a longshoreman on the Galveston waterfront. But he loved to cook and often prepared meals for his church functions. In 1955, he opened Sidney's Drive-Inn, located at 2605 Avenue G, or Winnie Street, directly behind the United States Courthouse. Sidney employed carhops to serve patrons in their cars and waitresses to serve customers who were seated in the small diner. The menu was simple and focused on traditional foods like hamburgers, cheeseburgers, French fries, root beer floats, milkshakes and a few other items. Sidney's advertised that its milk and ice cream were obtained locally from Galveston's Star Dairy. Star Dairy, together with Kobarg Dairy and Model Dairy, were Galveston's leading dairies in the 1950s.

Neighbors would walk blocks to the "Big Burger House," as it was called by some, to purchase juicy hamburgers. Others remember meeting up at Sidney's after Central High football games or for Sunday-evening getaways to meet friends for burgers and a milkshake. After Sidney's Drive-Inn closed in 1966, the building was torn down. Melvin Sidney died at the age of eighty-five on July 5, 2004. His survivors included his children, Melvin Sidney Jr., Alfred Sidney, Dorothy Ann Allen, Patricia Ellis and Grace Jones.

LIZA'S SOUL FOOD

Eliza Mae Gipson was one of fourteen brothers and sisters who grew up on a sugarcane and peanut farm in Minter, Alabama. She was born on May 5, 1929, and by the age of six, her grandmother had put a spoon in her hand and directed her to the stove in what proved to be the beginning of her culinary training. When Liza was older, she came to Galveston to visit a sick aunt and happened to meet Precious Gipson. Precious Gipson Sr. was born on November 16, 1916, in Trinity County, Texas.

After Eliza and Precious were married, Precious opened Gipson's Place at 2720 Market Street, which he operated for over twenty-five years. In the late 1960s, Eliza opened Liza's Soul Kitchen across the street at 2723 Market Street. The restaurant remained open until the middle of the 1980s. While Precious provided adult beverages in his place to their clientele, Eliza cooked authentic soul food across the street, including some of her specialties, like oxtails, mustard greens, rice and gravy. The peach cobbler was legendary, and customers often pre-ordered entire cobblers to take home. Over the years, Eliza was often asked what the most important thing to remember about cooking was. She always replied: "You've got to pay attention to what you are doing! That's what makes a good cook!"

Customer Larry Parson remembers that the plates at the restaurant included a main course of pork chops, fried chicken or oxtails and included greens, rice and gravy and macaroni and cheese. He fondly remembers playing basketball at Wright Cuney Park with the Gipsons' sons. Retired Galveston County banker Edward Patton recalls the bowling leagues at Gulf Bowling Lanes and how Liza's Soul Kitchen never failed to sponsor a team and always provided a complimentary meal to the team that won the league championship.

The oldest of the Gipson children was Willis Alexander. He believes his mother's restaurant was the first soul food café on the island. The restaurant capitalized on the laborers working on Galveston's waterfront and was in proximity to the International Longshoremen's Association halls number 851 and 329. It also delivered meals to Todd's Shipyard, and Willis vividly remembers making trips to Pelican Island to deliver lunch and dinner to the workers at Todd's. The smothered steak and the pepper steak were two of the most popular menu items at Liza's. According to Willis, "She had the best pepper steak, and it was popular among the regular customers." He also recalled that the restaurant sold out of food on most days. Preston Gipson believes his mom had the best food in town. He recalls that when the siblings arrived home from school, they always sat down to a great supper. His fondest memory is his mother's sweet cornbread, which made a lasting impression. The restaurant received great reviews from KGBC-AM 1540 radio every evening on Sam Willoughby's show and later on Randy Sterling's show. According to Willis, "Mr. Sterling would always have something good to say about the food at Liza's." During a brief period, Eliza also cooked for her sister Hannah Hunter at the Soul Q Pit at 2602 Ball Street. The special every Wednesday was oxtails, and it received front-page coverage in the *Galveston County Daily News* on Saturday, November 11, 1995.

Precious Gipson passed away at St. Mary's Hospital in Galveston on October 10, 1985. The service was held at Mount Calvary Baptist Church, and he was buried at Broyal Chapel Cemetery in Riverside, Texas, under the direction of Fields Funeral Home. He was survived by his wife, Eliza, one daughter and five sons. He was also survived by twenty-five grandchildren and thirteen great-grandchildren. In May 2019, Eliza celebrated her ninetieth birthday. She still resides in Galveston and remains an active member of First Union Baptist Church in Galveston, where it is common to find her on Sunday mornings at worship with her daughter Jennifer.

In a *Galveston Daily News* article, retired managing editor Heber Taylor once mentioned, "Great cooks tend to be like great artists, they have a dim view of performing by numbers, recipes or formulas." Eliza Gipson was certainly a culinary artist for the record books.

Eliza Gipson's Oxtails

1. Trim the oxtails.
2. Put the oxtails in pan and season with salt, pepper and secret things.
3. Add onions and bell pepper.
4. Cover the pan with foil to keep the savory steam in.
5. Cook at about 400 degrees in oven for 3 to 4 hours.

Chapter 3

Pit Stops

Galveston Barbecue Restaurants

Texans have an undeniable infatuation with barbecue. The English word *barbecue* and cognates in other languages come from the Spanish word *barbacoa*. A *Time* magazine article, "The History of Barbecue," identified four styles of barbecue: Memphis, Kansas City, North Carolina and, of course, Texas.

Since the 1930s, Galveston citizens have had many restaurants specializing in barbecued meats to choose from, with no shortage of discussions and arguments about who was the best of all time (BOAT). It's an appropriate acronym for a town situated along the edge of the Gulf of Mexico.

The census for the city of Galveston in 1930 recorded 52,938 people. The African American population stood at 13,226, or 24.98 percent of the city's total, according to statistics found in the Galveston City Directory that year.

The presence of Jim Crow laws and segregation made it necessary for African American–owned and operated businesses to serve the African American community. Barbecue was always a popular meal. The 1992 movie *Fried Green Tomatoes* and its depiction of a barbecue pit behind the Whistle Stop Café is probably not too far from Galveston's reality in the 1930s.

Nelson "Honey" Brown was given the unofficial title "Galveston's King of Barbecue." It is a distinction worthy of the honor. There was plenty of competition for that recognition. Listed below are several barbecue restaurants that opened for only a short period of time amid strong competition. They surely contributed to the discussion of great plates. While it is not a complete list, it does acknowledge the eagerness of individuals to show off their culinary skills.

HONEY BROWN BAR-B-QUE

Nelson "Honey" Brown was born in Gainesmore, Texas, on November 7, 1907. The small community, also known as At Last, was a stop on the Southern Pacific Railroad. It was located south of Bay City in eastern Matagorda County on Caney Creek. In 1950, the town was abandoned.

In 1926, Honey Brown moved to Galveston. The move was described by his family and friends as an opportunity "to seek a place for himself." After he arrived, Brown worked at Perthius Wholesale Produce, at 2010 Strand, in the historic Hendley Building. Brown settled down, made Galveston his home and, in 1947, opened a barbecue restaurant at 2728 Church. Gus Allen owned the building and leased the space to him.

The restaurant opened in 1947 as Honey's Barbecue, but the name was quickly changed to Honey's Café. In the 1960s, the name changed again to Honey's Bar-B-Que Pit before Brown finally settled on Honey Brown Bar-B-Que. For a period during the restaurant's operation, the business was open twenty-four hours a day. Customers and friends said you could smell the aroma of Honey's barbecue anytime, day or night. During the 1950s and the Jim Crow era, Honey's barbecue crossed racial boundaries, creating friendships forged through the common enjoyment and appreciation of outstanding barbecue.

Honey Brown quickly became known as Galveston's "King of Barbecue." It might have been an unofficial title, but the legend grew over the years. The 1927 Traub Manufacturing slogan, "Often imitated but never duplicated," could have been applied to Brown's sauce. Brown called the sauce "teased and pleased." He never revealed the ingredients for the sauce or for his special barbecue rub during his lifetime. In 1990, *Galveston Daily News* reporter Maury Darst interviewed Brown's widow, Edna Earl Brown, who admitted that Brown never even told her how he made his barbecue rub and sauce. In addition to their barbecue, Honey Brown's customers could order cold soft drinks. Side orders included potato salad and pork and beans. Miss Edna, Honey's wife and the main cook, added sugar to the beans to make them "extra special." She was also responsible for the desserts. Banana pudding and apple pie were the customers' favorites.

When you mention Honey Brown to anyone who ate there, the reaction is always the same. Everyone smiles as they recall their unique memories about the restaurant and the food. Longtime Galveston resident and local businessman Ransom Lundy still states without hesitation that the barbecued ribs were the best he ever had. He recalls that he ordered ribs

Inside Honey Brown Bar-B-Que restaurant. Gus Allen stands at the end of the counter. *Courtesy Rosenberg Library, Galveston, Texas.*

nearly every time but remembers that the sausage links and brisket were also crowd favorites. Lundy smiles when he talks about the times he visited Honey Brown's pit. The memory creates an excitement that those who did not eat there cannot fully understand. Gilbert Zamora Jr., who grew up in Galveston and graduated from Ball High School in 1953, remembered eating at Honey's in the 1950s. Zamora recalled times his coworkers would go by Honey Brown's and bring barbecue back to the National Marine Fisheries. He also mentioned how his uncle would stop by the restaurant and pick up barbecue for his family.

Former Galveston resident Bill Cherry shared his beloved memories of Honey's Bar-B-Que in an article featured in the *Galveston Daily News* in March 2002. The article provided a lengthy description of the brisket sandwich that Cherry ordered often from Honey's. Simply made with fresh white bread piled high with tender brisket and onions and smothered in Honey's sweet barbecue sauce, the sandwich was served wrapped in butcher paper. Cherry remembered eating the sandwich with Fritos corn chips while he sipped a

Coca-Cola and listened to rhythm and blues music. By Cherry's standards, that combination made for an unbeatable Saturday night in 1956. During the 1970s, local resident Barbara Sanderson remembered eating at Honey's with her father, Galveston Police detective Oscar Ekelund. Sanderson was a student in junior high at the time and recalled fondly that her favorite place to sit and eat her brisket was beside the huge barbecue pit.

At Thanksgiving and Christmas each year, in addition to the day-to-day operations of the restaurant, Brown catered holiday parties. Local families could bring raw meats for Honey to season with his secret rub before he cooked them to order. The restaurant operated around the clock in order to ensure that everyone's holiday orders were taken care of. Customers recalled that menu items were priced to favor patrons over profit and that Brown did not throw away any scrap of food, as he did not like to see anyone go hungry. When he had the opportunity to feed someone who couldn't afford the meal, Brown fed them. The recipient of his kind gesture often performed small chores around the restaurant in gratitude. Miss Edna often joked that he gave away more than he sold.

A glimpse into Honey Brown's life reveals nothing unusual. He was a member of Macedonia Baptist Church and loved dogs, especially his German shepherd, named "Gus" in honor of his business rival and friend Gus Allen. Brown was not fond of the storms that rolled in off the Gulf of Mexico. At the first sign of thunder or lightning, he would calmly walk into a closet and wait until the storm passed. There was no negotiating with him during a storm; he was not going to budge. The local newspaper frequently reported on happenings at the restaurant or with the King of Barbecue himself. In February 1960, burning grease in the barbecue oven caused a fire at the restaurant. A second fire in September 1975 gutted the building. Firefighters extinguished the blaze before it spread to an adjacent building. Both incidents were reported in the local newspaper. Also in 1975, Brown was hospitalized. His recovery made the community section of the local newspaper. Well-wishers hoped that Brown was back at his place of glory soon, reigning over the pit.

Honey Brown passed away in Galveston on February 27, 1979. He was survived by his wife, Edna Earl, a sister and two brothers. He was interred at Galveston's Lakeview Cemetery. Honey had been a resident of Galveston for more than fifty years. The legacy of his famous barbecue has faded, but whenever it is mentioned to anyone who ate at his restaurant, the conclusion is universal: it was the best barbecue anyone ever tasted, and no barbecue since has come close to matching it. For a span of more than thirty years,

Nelson "Honey" Brown Jr. was known as Galveston's barbecue king. His accomplishment as a great barbecue pit master left a legacy that set the standard for those who followed.

GALVESTON BAR-B-Q PIT

Walter Collins was born on January 15, 1918, in Clarence, Louisiana. He opened his restaurant, the Galveston Bar-B-Q Pit, in 1957 at 2609 Market. In 1972, he moved the restaurant to 2708 Market. The Galveston Bar-B-Q Pit was a popular place to eat ribs, brisket and homemade sausage links. Collins did what was necessary to be available for his customer base and was noted for staying open until 3:30 a.m. in the late 1960s and early 1970s to accommodate workers on the waterfront. People around town talked about the tenderness of the brisket and ribs that came off of Collins's pit. Collins and his employees came up with a slang phrase that complimented the texture of their meat: "You need no teeth to eat the beef." After hearing that, anyone with an appetite and a curiosity paid Walter Collins a visit.

According to Collins's nephew James Collins, it took some convincing to get his uncle to add rib sandwiches to the restaurant's menu. Concerned about the expense of the sandwich and whether or not his customer base would be willing to pay the extra cost, Collins eventually added the sandwich. It proved to be the restaurant's best seller and often sold out completely on busy weekends.

In 1962, James began to spend time with his uncle in the restaurant, observing his uncle's specific barbecue style. James attended public schools in Houston and Los Angeles. He graduated from Los Angeles Freemont High School in 1973 and moved to Galveston in 1976 to work for his uncle at the restaurant. James moved back to California and, in 1983, opened the second location of the Galveston Bar-B-Q Pit in Compton, California. James educated the California staff on how to prepare the barbecue based on knowledge his Uncle Walter taught him. With two locations open in Texas and California, Galveston Bar-B-Q Pit fit the definition of a chain restaurant, with more than one location operating under the same name and selling similar merchandise.

The Galveston Bar-B-Q location in California closed in 1991. Walter Collins continued to operate the Galveston location until his death in 1992. Collins was a Galveston resident for forty-six years and a veteran of World

War II. He is interred at Lakeview Cemetery in Galveston. James assumed ownership of the Galveston Bar-B-Q Pit after his uncle's death. He kept the restaurant open until 1994, when he closed it and moved back to California.

In 2013, James returned to Galveston, where he still carries his Uncle Walter Collins's barbecue legacy. He uses his uncle's technique for each type of meat he puts on the pit. His favorite meats to smoke include brisket (lean or marbled), pork ribs, chicken and homemade sausage links. He is most proud of his smoked burger with handmade patties seasoned to perfection before they hit the pit. Collins is a throwback and possesses the old-school values of a generation that took pride in its work. In culinary terms, the lifetime journey to perfect his own barbecue skills that Walter Collins started his nephew on has paid off as a job well done.

IXL BARBECUE

Ophelia Rice Benjamin was known to be a great cook. However, family and friends raved about her barbecue more than anything else. They looked forward to an invitation to the Benjamins' home, especially when the menu was barbecue. So, in 1961, Ophelia's husband, William, found a building that had previously been a barbecue restaurant to set his wife up with a place where they could sell her popular barbecue.

William Benjamin was born on June 27, 1914, in the village of McNary, Louisiana. His family moved to Houston, Texas, when he was a teenager. Ophelia Rice was born on August 8, 1915, and raised in Houston, Texas. The two met in Houston while attending Wheatley High School. After they graduated, the couple got married in 1935. William had several small jobs, but as his young family grew, he sought better employment. In 1939, he moved his family to Galveston Island, where he found employment at an iron and metal company. Their home was located at the rear of 2810 Avenue I (Sealy), along the alley. Ophelia cared for the house and the couple's five children, Lena, Rosalind, Edward, Doris and Alice. While she worked as a housewife, she perfected her cooking skills preparing dishes inspired by family recipes.

In 1961, William decided his wife should sell her famous barbecue. He leased a building at 2727 Postoffice Street that had previously housed a restaurant, IXL Barbecue. In addition to the commercial space on the ground floor, the building provided living accommodations for the Benjamin family

IXL Barbecue owners William and Ophelia Benjamin celebrate a wedding anniversary. *Courtesy Benjamin family.*

adjacent to and above the restaurant. While William worked at the iron and metal company and his second, part-time job on the docks, Ophelia ran the family restaurant with help from the couple's daughter Doris. Still in high school, Doris worked in the restaurant after school. Later, the Benjamins' niece Denise, whom they raised, entered the family business. IXL's hours were 3:00 p.m. to 10:00 p.m. on weekdays and 12:00 p.m. to 11:00 p.m. on weekends. While William enjoyed the barbecue, when he came to the restaurant after work, Ophelia always had a special meal prepared for him. Family remembered that his favorite dish was liver and onions.

IXL Barbecue sold pork ribs, veal, chicken, homemade sausage links, potato salad, pinto beans and soft drinks. Customers could dine in or pick up their orders to go. The barbecue plates included the customer's choice of one meat, plus a piece of chicken or a sausage link and two sides. Items could also be purchased by the pound.

Denise remembered her Aunt Ophelia seasoning the chicken, veal and pork ribs with Cajun spices and garlic, onion and lemon juice. Ophelia

The Benjamins' daughter Rosalind poses with cousins on a car parked in front of their parents' establishment, which was located at 2727 Postoffice. Date unknown. *Courtesy Benjamin family*.

always made the sausage links, and no one could remember the ingredients she used. But, being observant, Denise could recall the recipes for the restaurant's potato salad and barbecue sauce. In order to make enough for the restaurant, she remembered her Aunt Ophelia tripled the recipes.

IXL Potato Salad

2 large Irish potatoes
2 stalks celery
1 small dill pickle
2 eggs
½ cup yellow onion
1 cup mayonnaise
1 tablespoon mustard

Directions:
Peel and cut each potato into six pieces and boil until tender (test with fork). Boil eggs. While potatoes and eggs boil, in a bowl mix together coarsely chopped celery, finely chopped pickle, finely chopped onion, mayonnaise and mustard. When cool, add potatoes and chopped eggs to mixture and mix thoroughly. Refrigerate.

IXL Barbecue Sauce

2 crushed garlic cloves
2 8-ounce cans tomato sauce
1 6-ounce can tomato paste
¾ cup cider vinegar
¾ cup firmly packed brown sugar
2 tablespoons prepared mustard
2 tablespoons oil
2 teaspoons salt
½ teaspoon pepper

Directions:
Sauté garlic in oil on medium heat and add remaining ingredients. Mix well. Boil gently uncovered for 30 minutes.

Equipment used to make the sausage served at IXL, still treasured by the Benjamin family. *Courtesy Benjamin family.*

On weekends, customers reserved the restaurant for parties and other celebrations. For private parties, the restaurant provided the food and guests were allowed to BYOB—bring in their own alcoholic beverages. William was present when these events occurred. After hours, when liquor stores were closed and customers desired more liquor, the Benjamin's daughter Rosalind remembered her father would ask her to "go get the little man"—a half pint of Johnnie Walker Scotch Whiskey—which he stocked and sold for a two-dollar profit.

In 1967, the Benjamins moved to Texas City, fifteen miles northwest of Galveston. By then, all of the Benjamin children were adults and on their own, except Denise. While they lived in Texas City, the daily commute to Galveston was a challenge for Ophelia, and she closed IXL Barbecue later that same year. Why the name IXL, one may ask? To this day, the meaning remains a mystery!

FIGGINS BARBECUE

Alfred L. Figgins was born in Franklin, Louisiana, on November 20, 1893. He enlisted in the United States Army and was a veteran of World War I. After he was discharged from the service, he returned home and relocated to the Beaumont–Port Arthur–Orange region of Texas, known as the Golden Triangle, a reference to the wealth that came from the Spindletop oil strike in Beaumont in 1901.

In the early 1920s, Figgins was briefly married to Grace Richard, with whom he shared a daughter, and later, he married Blanche Johnson. Johnson was born on October 7, 1907, in Orange, Texas, where she also attended school. Their union had nine children. In 1931, the couple moved the family to Galveston, where Figgins managed the Harlem Inn Restaurant and later worked as a porter at Island Motors on Tremont Street. By the 1940s, city directories noted his occupation as a laborer. In the same period, with a growing family, Figgins made the courageous and strategic move into the restaurant business when he opened Figgins Barbecue Stand at the family residence at 613 Thirty-Fifth Street. Soon after the family's restaurant opened, they experienced a heartbreaking tragedy when their teenage son Alfred Jr. lost his life in a swimming accident off Twenty-Eighth and Seawall. As the family mourned, they continued to build the foundation for a successful barbecue business. By 1946, Figgins had built a customer base that allowed the family to move the business away from their home and expand and open two new venues, at 514 Twenty-Sixth Street and 2302 Twenty-Eighth Street. Alfred operated one location, and Blanche, soon known affectionately as "Big Mama," operated the second site.

In 1948, the family decided on one location for the barbecue stand. The two storefronts merged and relocated to 617 Twenty-Sixth Street. As the children grew older, they received an education on how to prepare authentic barbecue. Gilbert Walker Figgins remembered that he learned the secrets of cooking good barbecue as a teenager. He cultivated that knowledge and was known during his lifetime for his skills as a barbecue pit master.

In 1952, the Galveston City Directory listing for Figgins Barbecue Stand promoted "old fashioned" pit barbecue. The listing also noted that the restaurant offered citywide deliveries and catered to private parties and banquets. Later that year, the business relocated for a final time and returned to 514 Twenty-Sixth Street. Figgins operated there until he closed the restaurant in 1954 and moved his family across the Galveston Causeway to La Marque.

After he relocated the family to La Marque, Figgins began to experience health problems. He passed away on March 26, 1956, at the Veterans Administration Hospital in Houston. He was survived by his wife, Blanche, five daughters, four sons, three sisters and sixteen grandchildren. He is interred at Mainland Memorial Cemetery in Hitchcock, Texas.

Blanche Figgins eventually moved back to Galveston and became an active member of Mount Moriah Baptist Church. Her younger brother Phillip Johnson opened King's Inn Restaurant in 1956. Blanche helped with the business that operated for over twenty years. The topic of Figgins Barbecue was brought up quite often by those who visited King's Inn for a meal. Blanche settled into her role as "Big Mama" at King's Restaurant and managed the business while she raised her family. Her role in the community took on an additional responsibility as she took interest in the neighborhood children. Whether it was a complimentary bite to eat, an encouraging word or a wave and smile, the local children felt that Big Mama always watched out for them.

As her service in the restaurant business came to an end for the second time, Blanche moved to a new arena. She took on an active role to increase the membership of Mount Moriah Baptist Church. Those who grew up in the congregation remember her influence and the significant change she made in the church community.

In 1997, Blanche "Big Mama" Figgins celebrated her ninetieth birthday. She died on January 3, 2001, in Galveston, Texas. She was preceded in death by her husband, Alfred, her parents, 2 brothers, 5 children, 3 grandchildren and 2 great-grandchildren. Her survivors included 2 sons, 3 daughters, 49 grandchildren, 113 great-grandchildren, 45 great-great-grandchildren and a great many loving friends. A tribute to her life appeared in the *Galveston County Daily News* on January 11, 2001. Civil rights icon Jackie Robinson once said, "A life is not important except in the impact it has on other lives." Blanche Figgins passed that test. In fact, you can say she aced the test. *Eternal rest* is an appropriate term for someone who worked tirelessly to help others for ninety-three years. Blanche Figgins and her beloved husband, Alfred, left a lasting legacy. There are a lot of citizens who were not born when Figgins Barbecue Stand was in operation, but they undoubtedly heard the stories passed down to the next generation regarding the restaurant and the family. Both left an indelible mark on the lives of many Galveston citizens.

OLIVER'S BAR-B-Q STAND

Marion Oliver Sr. was born on May 16, 1910, in Navasota, Texas, located seventy-one miles northwest of Houston. The youngest of three children, Oliver moved to Galveston with his family when he was sixteen years old. As a teenager, he worked small jobs to help the family and first found consistent employment at Todd Dry Dock and later as a merchant seaman. Lucinda "Lucy" Davis was born on January 2, 1909, in Jeanerette, Louisiana, the oldest of twelve children. Her family worked the crops in the fields of Jeanerette, thirty-five miles southeast of Lafayette, Louisiana. Her father moved the Davis family to Galveston to seek better employment when Lucinda was thirteen or fifteen years old. It's unknown when Lucinda and Oliver met, but they married in 1929. Their home was located at 3613 M ½ Street and later at Thirty-Fourth Street and Avenue N. To their union one son was born, Marion Oliver Jr. It was a blended family, with Lucinda's two sons by a previous union, Floyd and Norvell Phillips, as well as one of Oliver's nieces, who also resided with the family.

After his retirement as a merchant seaman, Oliver Sr. purchased a two-story building at 614 Thirty-Fifth Street in 1945 and opened a "beer joint," where he sold beer and soft drinks on the first floor. The family lived above the club, which he named Oliver's. At the back of the building's first floor was an old barbecue pit. Lucinda was the one who suggested the club should sell barbecue. The couple combined their families' barbecue recipes and changed the name of the business to Oliver's Bar-B-Q Stand. Neither Oliver Jr. nor Oliver III knew why it was named a "stand," because all customers were served indoors.

Oliver III remembered his grandma Lucy was "the boss" who ran the business, and Oliver Jr. agreed. The restaurant's menu included veal, pork ribs, chicken, homemade sausage links, pinto beans, potato salad and barbecue sauce. It also sold beer and soft drinks but never any desserts. For several years, the restaurant was open twenty-four hours a day. After a few years, the operating hours were changed to 11:00 a.m. to 6:00 a.m., Tuesday through Sunday.

Oliver Jr. began to work at the restaurant when he was eight years old. He worked after school and on weekends cleaning up and performing other chores as his mother directed. When he got a little older, he deboned the quarter calves that his father purchased, washed the casing for the sausage links, ground the beef and pork for the sausage links and helped his mother monitor whatever was on the pit. Oliver Sr. also monitored the pit, but Lucy was always in charge.

The Olivers' barbecue pit had a firebox where oak, pecan or hickory wood was burned to cook the meat, chicken and sausage links. Everything was seasoned with a dry rub before it went on the pit. Once the items were seared on all sides over the fire, they were moved away from the heat and periodically mopped with a liquid mixture until done. An inquiry for the dry-rub seasoning mixture brought silence from Oliver Jr. and Oliver III. However, without offering the quantity, they shared the ingredients for the

Above: Marion Oliver Sr. sits inside his restaurant and visits with customers. *Courtesy Oliver family.*

Left: Lucinda "Lucy" Davis Oliver. Family members fondly recall that Miss Lucy was the true boss of the business. *Courtesy Oliver family.*

Meat smoking on the pit behind Oliver's Bar-B-Q Stand. *Courtesy Oliver family.*

rub and mop mixture; the rub included salt, pepper and paprika. After cooking a while, the items were mopped with a simmered mixture of onions, peppers, lemon juice and water. Oliver Jr. remembered that the meat was turned often and noted they "never use a fork to turn the meat." There was no timer or meat thermometer; doneness was determined by sight and touch. Oliver III volunteered the ingredients (without measurements) for the family's potato salad: boiled potatoes, finely chopped celery, bell pepper, garlic and onion mixed with mayonnaise, mustard, pickle relish, vinegar, paprika and cayenne pepper. Once blended, the salad was refrigerated before serving. The recipe never included boiled eggs. In the 1940s and '50s, a barbecue sandwich cost $1.50 and a plate with veal, ribs, quarter chicken or a link with potato salad and pinto beans cost $5.00. The "regular," one of the most ordered items, was a sandwich that included a combination of scrapings or bits of meat that fell on the table when cutting the veal, ribs or chicken. The sandwich was served with barbecue sauce and, in the '40s, sold for 25¢. In the 1950s, the price increased to 50¢.

Oliver's Bar-B-Q Stand also had a jukebox and a pool table that made it a popular hangout for the local crowd. Customers held parties and celebrations at the restaurant and were able to BYOB—bring their own bottles. The restaurant provided food and "set-ups." Oliver III recalled that Lucy enjoyed the events as much as the guests did. He noted, "My grandmother was a party girl." To make sure the fun continued after liquor stores closed, Oliver Sr. stocked half pints of liquor, including Canadian Club Whiskey, Seagram's Gin, Crown Royal Whiskey and W.L. Weller

From left to right: Marion Oliver III, Marion Oliver Jr. and Marion Oliver Sr. *Courtesy Oliver family*.

Bourbon. He purchased the half pints at a liquor store and sold them for two to three dollars more. Oliver III commented, "My grandfather made the owner of that liquor store rich."

The best party every year was Oliver Sr.'s birthday party. He celebrated his birthday the entire month of May and would purchase two goats or wild turkeys, often both, a few months before. Oliver Sr. fattened them up for weeks before he barbecued them on the pit. His party was open to the public, day and night. Regular menu items were also sold during the party month. Oliver Jr. recalled that his father was always generous, giving food to needy families or money to purchase groceries or pay rent.

Jerry Warren remembered his father taking him to Oliver's Bar-B-Que while growing up. His dad, A.J. Warren Jr., owned Warren's Plumbing and Heating. Jerry remembered the pit was inside and how good it smelled when one entered the building. The Warrens loved the brisket. When Warren Jr. passed away in 1972 at his residence, Oliver Sr. prepared barbecue for all of those who attended the service. According to Jerry Warren: "He did that out of the kindness of his heart. It was totally unexpected, but not out of character for Mr. Oliver Sr." He had a big heart and mourned the passing of his friend.

Oliver III followed in his father's footsteps and started to work at the restaurant when he was eight years old, assigned some of the same chores his father performed as a boy. He worked weekends and holidays, and after he enrolled in college, Oliver III worked at the restaurant whenever he was home, recollecting how "it was nice to have a little change in my pocket." His sister Lisa Oliver never worked at the restaurant.

Lucinda Oliver passed away in 1983. Oliver Sr. maintained the business, and when he became ill, Oliver Jr. took over the business. As the years passed, the clientele decreased. Oliver Jr. closed the business in 1996. Two years later, Marion Oliver Sr. passed, on August 23, 1998.

FLEMING'S

Ed Fleming was the owner of Fleming's Bar-B-Q Pit. He was born on October 3, 1902, in Wharton County, Texas. His cemetery marker lists his date of birth as October 2, 1895, but the death certificate issued by Galveston County recorded the date as October 3, 1902. Fleming's first attempt in the food business started in 1938 at 2309 Twenty-Ninth Street.

By 1943, the restaurant was closed. He reopened the business again around 1951 at the same location. In late 1952 or early 1953, Fleming moved the establishment nine blocks north, to 1401 Twenty-Ninth Street, in proximity to both Macedonia Baptist Church and Shiloh African Methodist Episcopal Church. It was a prime spot and easily accessible to those who wanted to stop by after services to pick up some tasty barbecue for Sunday dinner at home.

The classified advertising section of the *Galveston Daily News* on December 9, 1952, advertised Fleming's Restaurant's barbecued wild game, meat and poultry. The restaurant offered special prices on all orders. The catering service and to-go orders were the largest volume of the business, as there were few regular sit-down customers. The location served the public through the 1950s.

As a student attending Central High School, Reverend Jerry Temple remembered groups of young men going to Fleming's at lunch to bring back barbecue to the young women they wanted to impress. Curtis Alex gave high marks for the blood sausage and boudin sausage served at Fleming's.

On November 9, 1960, Edward Fleming died from injuries sustained in an automobile accident. He was survived by his wife, Zennie, son, Randolph, and daughters Mary L. Hughes, Nora Lee Martin and Bernice Williams. His service was held at the Taylor Funeral Home, followed by interment at Galveston's Memorial Cemetery.

After Fleming's death, Alfred Edwards took over the location and opened Edward D's Barbecue in 1962. In 1964, Johnny O'Bryant took over management, and by 1967, the name of the restaurant had changed to Clemmen's Barbeque. In 1969, the establishment was still under management of O'Bryant, but the name had changed to Uncle Johnny's Tavern, ending the building's more than twenty years hosting a barbecue establishment. Today, no traces of Fleming's Bar-B-Q Pit exist. The restaurant and surrounding buildings were demolished years ago. The land was converted into a parking lot for Shiloh Church, dedicated to the loving memory of church trustee Vertrail Thompson.

LONE STAR BARBECUE PIT

Lone Star Barbecue Pit was initially located at 1114 Twenty-Eighth Street. The establishment was owned and operated by Earnest Rosenett. Rosenett was born in Baldwin, Louisiana, on August 3, 1897, and made his move from Louisiana to Galveston in the middle of the 1920s.

Rosenett opened the Lone Star Barbecue Pit in the late 1940s on Twenty-Eighth Street, between Avenues K and L. During a brief period in the late 1940s and early 1950s, a second diner with the same name operated at 3204 Ball. The 1949 Galveston City Directory noted the owner as Lillian Alvia and, in 1951, as Vernel Roberts. By 1953, this business was no longer included in the directory. During its years of operation, it bore no affiliation with Rosenett.

After operating at 1114 Twenty-Eighth Street for over ten years, Rosenett moved his barbecue pit a few blocks east in 1960 and settled the business at 1201 Twenty-Sixth Street. Customers remember that he was fair and always willing to extend credit to those in need.

Lifetime Galveston resident Larnell Mitchell Jr. remembered eating at Lone Star Barbecue Pit when he was a kid and recalled the barbecued sausage-link sandwich in particular. The sausage links were made in-house, tied at the end with a small piece of string and put on the pit. The sandwich was simply made using two slices of white bread and the restaurant's signature homemade barbecue sauce. The sandwich was wrapped in a section of the local newspaper and placed in a brown paper bag. Freddie Mea Scott remembered eating at Lone Star Barbecue when it first opened in the late 1940s. She grew up in Galveston and ate barbecue at other locations, but Lone Star was always her first choice.

Lone Star Barbecue's sauce was a favorite. Rosenett was asked many times to reveal how he made the sauce, but he kept his recipe a secret. Rosenett's brisket and ribs had great flavor and were popular plates, but his signature item was his homemade sausage links. His loyal customers proclaimed them the best barbecue links in town. Curtis Alex remembered how good the blood sausage, boudin and venison sausages were. All links were made fresh daily and were the common denominator that brought customers back to the restaurant. Alex also gave credit to the cooks who put in the extra effort to prepare the extraordinary meals for the customers.

Rosenett, a Galveston resident for over thirty-seven years, managed the Lone Star Barbecue Pit until he died in January 1962. Strode Funeral Home directed the service. He was laid to rest at Baldwin Cemetery in Baldwin, Louisiana. His survivors included his wife, Othelia, son Edward and a daughter, Ora Valory.

Othelia kept the business open after his death. She sold the restaurant in 1966 to Charley Compton, who began a new era at Lone Star Barbecue. By

1968, Compton had changed the name to the Lone Star Barbecue Stand. Charley was born on March 7, 1917, in Cheneyville, Louisiana. He was a veteran of World War II and a longtime resident of Galveston County. He operated the Lone Star Barbecue Stand until he sold it to James Foster in 1972, but by 1974, Compton had regained ownership. After Compton reacquired the barbecue pit, his brother Henry Compton became involved with the business. Henry split time between the docks, where he worked as a longshoreman, and the barbecue stand.

Henry Compton was born on June 14, 1932, in Lyles, Louisiana. He attended Jerusalem Baptist Church and was a member of the International Longshoremen's Association Local 20 and Amity Lodge Number 4 F&AM. In June 1974, Henry married Jann Thompson at Shiloh AME Church. Jann had the management skills required to operate the restaurant and, in 1976, took control of the establishment and allowed Henry more time to earn a living as a longshoreman.

In February 1979, a fire next door to the restaurant caused significant damage to the building. It had to undergo a full renovation that took years before the restaurant could reopen. During the repairs, the barbecue pit was moved outside the building, along with additional upgrades required by the county health department, including multiple sinks in the kitchen area and restroom facilities located inside the establishment. The restaurant reopened under the name Lone Star Kitchen, and in 1981, Jann Thompson Compton was still in charge. The reopening brought a change in format, too. Lone Star Kitchen sold home-cooked dinners and alcoholic beverages. The change allowed the restaurant to remain competitive and regain its customer base that had moved after the fire.

Jann Compton once stated that she and her staff decided what to cook each day. In the late 1980s, she sold the restaurant to Alvin Stephenson. Under Stephenson's management, the Lone Star remained open for a short period before Stephenson closed the restaurant permanently.

Charley Compton passed away in 1985. He was survived by his wife, Bernice, eight sons, four daughters, thirty-two grandchildren, one great-grandchild, three brothers and five sisters. He was buried at Mainland Memorial Cemetery in Hitchcock. Henry Compton passed away in 1991. He was buried at Galveston's Lakeview Cemetery. He was survived by two sons, five sisters, two brothers and his wife, Jann.

Lone Star Barbecue operated for almost forty years. Multiple name changes, different locations and several management turnovers created a lot of good memories for a lot of good people. The restaurant's loyal

Lone Star Barbecue building, on the corner of Twenty-Sixth Street and Avenue L.

customer base remembers and respects the legacy of both the Rosenett and Compton families. Jann Compton still resides in Galveston. Her daily journeys often take her by the location where she spent much of her time in the 1970s and 1980s.

Johnson's Barbecue

In the early 1930s, Hollie McFadden operated a barbecue restaurant at 702 Twenty-Seventh Street. A few years after the restaurant opened, McFadden moved the business next door, to 704 Twenty-Seventh Street. She remained there until she closed the doors in 1938. In the early 1940s, the restaurant opened under new ownership. Known as Johnson's Barbecue, the restaurant was operated by William Turner until it closed in 1946.

ADAM'S BARBECUE PLACE

As the Depression continued, Matthew Bridges opened a barbecue joint at 714 Twenty-Seventh Street. By the middle of the 1930s, ownership of the restaurant had transferred to Wheeler and Norvella Adams. They changed the name to Adam's Barbecue Place and served the citizens of Galveston for over fifteen years. The business closed in the early 1950s. An advertisement in the *Galveston Examiner* on December 12, 1939, described Adam's Barbecue as "The Place of Good Foods."

MATTHEW'S CAFÉ

Dee Matthews was born in Bryan, Texas, on July 7, 1890. In the late 1920s, Matthews opened a cafe at 617 Twenty-Sixth Street, but he moved to 611 Twenty-Seventh Street soon after. By 1939, Matthew's Café was listed in the Galveston City Directory classified section under the heading "Barbecue." The café served the community until it closed in 1948. Matthews passed away on August 13, 1960. A resident of Galveston for thirty-nine years, he is buried at Memorial Cemetery in Hitchcock, Texas.

PRICE'S BARBECUE PIT

In the middle of the 1930s, James Price opened Price's Barbecue Pit at 2311 Twenty-Eighth Street. Although the restaurant had a prime location near the Seawall and beach, it was in business for just a few short years.

SNELL'S BARBECUE

Rebecca Snell opened Snell's Barbecue in the mid-1930s. Snell's restaurant was located at 104 Seventeenth Street, several blocks from the majority of the African American businesses during that time. Snell's was situated in proximity to the port, across the street from the wharves along Pier 17. Although she catered to the workforce, Rebecca was in business for only a few years. Snell was born in Beaumont, Texas, in 1906. She passed away in Galveston on January 5, 1957, and was buried at Galveston's Memorial Cemetery.

MAX'S BARBECUE STAND / A&C BARBECUE

In the early 1940s, Max's Barbecue Stand opened at 1401 Twenty-Ninth Street. Owned and operated by Columbus Heard, the restaurant closed in the fall of 1948. The location remained vacant for a short time before A&C Barbecue replaced it. Alex Thompson managed A&C for a few years before it closed. Ed Fleming moved in next and opened Fleming's Barbecue at the location. Fleming's thrived through the 1950s but closed in 1960.

OLD FASHIONED BARBECUE

Old Fashioned Barbecue was also open for a short time in the early 1940s. It was operated by A.W. Jackson and located at 2517 Market Street. The restaurant's listing in the 1941 Galveston City Directory noted a menu of barbecue and beer, with lunch specials available daily. The listing also promoted special rates for private parties.

DOYLE'S BARBECUE

James Doyle operated his barbecue pit and restaurant at 1114 Twenty-Eighth Street in the early 1940s. Freddie Mea Scott recalled stories about Mr. Doyle's barbecue and remembered that the business stayed open for just a few years. By the end of the decade, Lone Star Barbecue had opened at the location and the story of its great barbecue began.

TIPPIN-IN BARBECUE CAFÉ

In 1946, Joseph Gabriel opened the Tippin-In Café at 4023 Ball Street. By 1949, the café had relocated to 2904 Ball. With the move, Gabriel made the commitment to specialize in nothing but barbecue. The Tippin-In remained open a few more years before it closed in 1952. Gabriel was born in Jeanerette, Louisiana, in 1910 and was a resident of Galveston for over sixty-five years. He attended Holy Rosary Catholic Church and worked for the City of Galveston. He passed away in Galveston in 1986 and was buried at Mainland Memorial Cemetery in Hitchcock, Texas. He was survived by his wife, Ida, two sons and two brothers.

GRANTEL BARBECUE

Grantel Barbecue was located at 2727 Winnie Street. Drummie Smith opened the restaurant in the middle of the 1950s. Smith also operated the Grand Tell Grocery & Café on Twenty-Eighth Street. In the late 1950s, Johnnie Ford assumed management of the café. Grantel Barbecue remained open until 1960.

Chapter 4

Cafés and Confectioneries

BIG TREE CAFÉ

Ira Captain was born in Beaumont, Texas, on July 31, 1912. There is no record of when he arrived in Galveston, but he was here by 1944, when he married Rosa Lee Carter that July. The same year, Ira opened the Big Tree Café on the corner of Postoffice and Twenty-Seventh Streets. The building, located at 2702 Postoffice Street, had previously been occupied by Tony's Grill, so it was a ready-made business opportunity for the Captains.

Ira and Rosa operated the café together until 1947, when their marriage ended. The *Galveston Daily News* reported on April 8, 1947, that the couple's divorce was finalized and the result of the separation gave ownership of the Big Tree Café to Rosa. She made no changes until 1948, when she relocated the restaurant to a two-story building at 2701 Market Street that provided space downstairs for the café and apartments upstairs, where Rosa resided. The new location on Market was closer to the port and the factories and warehouses that surrounded it, making it easy for dockworkers to stop by whenever they were hungry. The sign at the café noted that Rosa offered both "short orders"—items that took little preparation time and moved quickly from kitchen to customer—and regular meals. The Big Tree remained at that location until it closed in 1952. By that time, Rosa had passed the day-to-day responsibilities and management of the café to Willie Ford. The building remained vacant for several years before the

2702 Postoffice Street, where Big Tree Café was once located.

Big Tree Café's sign, recently donated to Galveston Historical Foundation's Preservation Resource Center.

Show Place Grill opened in its place. After Rosa closed the café, she left Galveston. Nothing else is known about her.

On December 10, 1949, county court records in the *Galveston Daily News* noted a property transfer from Rosa to Ira Captain. The property was located at 3415 Ball and served as Ira Captain's residence well into the 1960s. After Rosa transferred the Galveston property to Ira, he and Ada Holloway were united in marriage in Harris County, Texas, on January 29, 1955. The newlyweds left Galveston and relocated to Houston, where they resided until they moved to Channelview, Texas. In 1999, Ira Captain passed away in Houston.

THE DOUBLE DIP

Evelyn Clarice Murphy Roberts was born in Galveston, Texas, on April 24, 1906. After her husband, Lawrence, died in 1943, she worked as a laundress at one of the local laundries until the early 1950s, when she opened the Double Dip Café on the corner of Ball and Fortieth Streets. Located at 3928 Ball, the café moved across the street to 3923 Ball Street in 1956, where it remained until it closed in 1959.

In the summer of 1959, Roberts opened another short-order café at 615 Forty-First Street. That café was initially known as Mrs. Roberts Café. Mary Scott worked at the café and remembered it was always busy, as Roberts served high-quality fast food at bargain prices. Prices were ideal for the times: hamburgers cost a quarter, fries were a dime, ice cream was a nickel and a penny would get you a homemade cookie. Pork chop sandwiches and other large sandwiches were forty cents. Conversations at the local high schools praised the great burgers at a great price. The location was only one block from the entrance to Wright Cuney Park, and it became a local hangout for the children, who could play music and dance while they waited on their order. Friday was always a busy day. According to David O'Neal, Roberts took care of the children and made up the difference when they didn't have enough money to pay for their visit.

In the early 1960s, Evelyn Roberts changed the name of the establishment to the Sugar Shack and maintained her reputation for great homemade hamburgers. In 1974, the Sugar Shack closed, ending Roberts's thirty-nine-year restaurant career. After she closed, Roberts's nephew Emmett Murphy Sr. lamented the loss of both the burgers and the pork chop sandwiches.

Evelyn Roberts died on July 22, 1983, at Danforth Memorial Hospital in Texas City, Texas. Her service was held at Macedonia Baptist Church in Galveston, under the direction of Fields Funeral Home, followed by interment at Memorial Cemetery in Galveston. She was survived by four sisters and two brothers. During the thirty-nine years she operated her restaurant, her kindness and generosity made a lasting impression on the community and especially on the countless children she encountered.

THE DRY DOCK CAFÉ

In 1943, Louisiana native Paul "Shinery" Shinette opened the Dry Dock Café at 2728 Postoffice Street, on the corner of Postoffice and Twenty-Eighth Streets. Shinette operated the café until he passed away on April 14, 1946, at John Sealy Hospital in Galveston. After his death, Lillian Atkins operated the café from 1946 until 1948. In 1948, the café changed management again, and "Miss Dorothy," Dorothy Antoine, became the new owner. Antoine was born in 1911 in Jeanerette, Louisiana, and under her management, the establishment's name changed to Antoine's Place. An advertisement for Antoine's in the 1952 Galveston City Directory described the restaurant as "One of Galveston's Finest Colored Cafés" and noted that it specialized in steaks, seafood and fried chicken. The advertisement also stated, "We never close."

In 1953, Sam Brown took over the business and changed its name to Brown's Place. He maintained the same advertisement in the city directory that Dorothy had used. By 1958, Brown had updated the ad to mention that the building had been "Air-Conditioned." Larry Parson, a 1972 graduate of Galveston Ball High School, has fond memories of the barbecue served at Brown's Place. The twenty-five-cent hamburgers were his favorite while growing up in the neighborhood. Parson remembers his older siblings sending him to Sam's to pick up their lunches. His courier fee for the trip was one hamburger. In 1959, Edward Young assumed ownership of the business; in 1964, ownership passed again, to Helen Carpell. By early 1966, Brown's Place had closed its doors.

Sam Brown died in Galveston in 1984. His obituary in the *Galveston Daily News* stated that he had been a café owner for more than forty years, had also worked as a masonry bricklayer and was a veteran of World War II. He was also a member of the Gus Allen American Legion Post 111, Post

No. 614, the Imperial Council of Nobles of the Mystic Shrine, the Elks Lodge, the Knights of Pythias of Texas, Queen City Lodge No. 11 and Zuliki Temple No. 7 D.O.K.O. He was also an associate member of the Texas Peace Officers Association.

The building at Postoffice and Twenty-Eighth Streets remained vacant until 1966, when Louise Smith opened the Louis Café. In late 1973, Mable White took up residency at 2728 Postoffice Street, and the name was changed to White's Grill. In late 1977, the establishment went through its final transition when the name changed to Hawaii Five-0 Restaurant, which operated until 1979.

The location where delicious meals were served to the public for over thirty years now sits vacant, and the building that once housed the many cafés has long been demolished. It is on a three-block strip of Postoffice Street that has been renamed Alfreda Houston Place. Houston was the executive director of the St. Vincent's House from 1975 until she retired in 1999 and received the *Galveston Daily News* Citizen of the Year award in 1997. Houston was married to Samuel Howard Houston for twenty-seven years. Her sister Edna Brown was married to Galveston Barbecue legend Nelson "Honey" Brown.

THE OLEANDER CAFÉ

The history of Oleander Café spanned more than forty years in Galveston. Records show that the restaurant operated at the corner of Thirty-Seventh and Church Streets as early as November 1921. The proprietor at that time was Zack Day. An advertisement printed in the *Galveston City Times* newspaper on November 11, 1921, described the Oleander Café as "the place for a good meal, fine cup of coffee and a good bowl of Chili."

The café transferred ownership sometime between 1926 and 1927 to Martha Leslie. The menu basically remained the same, with a few of Leslie's specialties added. An advertisement in the *Galveston Sentinel* noted that Leslie baked all of the pastries served at the café. Located on a corner, the café had two addresses, 3628 Church Street and 518 Thirty-Seventh Street. In June 1940, Martha Leslie married George Nickollson.

Overton "Obie" Parker became the proprietor of the café in the late 1940s. Parker was born in Saint Martinville, Louisiana, in 1898 or 1899. Under Parker's management, the Oleander Café moved across the street, to 611 Thirty-Seventh Street. Obie Parker loved sports as fiercely as any athlete,

The first location of the Oleander Café, on the corner of Church and Thirty-Seventh Streets.

according to longtime *Galveston Daily News* sportswriter Jimmy Blair. He had an important role in the Negro softball league that played on the Wright Cuney diamond and was also responsible for the construction of the softball field at Thirty-Third and Ball Streets. In later years, a heart attack slowed him physically, but it did not slow down his passion. Parker was instrumental in the development of the baseball league for African American youth and was a coach of the well-known Triple XXX Dodgers, a team sponsored by the Oleander Cafe. Later, he coached and helped sponsor the ILA 851 Falcons along with Louis Simpson. The success of the Galveston Central High School baseball program can be traced to Obie Parker. He worked tirelessly with the young players, and many of his teams won championships.

Ransom Lundy's funeral home was just a few blocks from the Oleander Café. Lundy recalled eating there on occasion and had high compliments for the food. Pork chops and fried chicken were popular menu items. According to David H. O'Neal, the café catered to a more subdued clientele and specialized in home cooking for breakfast, lunch and dinner with an emphasis on great seafood. It is said that the seafood or the shrimp platters were second to none

Oleander Café's second location, at 611 Thirty-Seventh Street.

in the city. The Oleander Café was also a regular meeting place for such organizations as the Galveston Negro Chamber of Commerce.

In 1960, John McBeth became the owner of the café, and it remained open for a few more years. On May 24, 1963, Overton "Obie" Parker passed away at St. Mary's Hospital in Galveston. By September 1963, the *Galveston Tribune* had noted that the Oleander Café was for sale and "equipped for immediate possession." The building remained vacant until 1965, when Rubin L. Jackson opened the Oleander Lounge at 611 Thirty-Seventh Street. Memories of the Oleander Café remain, however, as the establishment and owners left an impressive mark on the community.

ROSE'S CONFECTIONARY

Businessman John Ned Rose Sr. was born in Crowley, Louisiana, on September 2, 1897, and arrived in Galveston around 1920. In 1938, Rose opened a soft-drink fountain at 3427 Sealy. One block away, at 3501 Ball

Street, he also operated the Galveston Tavern, an establishment that sold adult beverages. Rose had the vision to expand, so, in the early 1950s, he opened a third business, Rose's Confectionary, located at 4402 Ball Street. An advertisement in the *Galveston News* announced the grand opening on July 14, 1951, and identified the establishment as "one of Galveston's most up-to-date confectionaries for the colored people of this city." The opening provided free ice cream for children and orchids to the first five hundred women attending the event.

Located near the Palm Terrace housing units, Rose's Confectionary offered a complete fountain service, over-the-counter drugs and other household needs. Rose's also served delicious pit barbecue daily, and at meal times, the shop was packed with people ordering food to go. The shop also offered locally made Purity Ice Cream. In his book *Galveston Memories*, former Galveston resident Bill Cherry describes how Purity Ice Cream owner G.B. Brynston marketed distribution of the ice cream by providing local businesses with freezers at cost. At a time when most local drugstores, grocery stores and confectioneries were family owned, this worked well for both parties.

According to grandson John Ned Rose III, in addition to ice cream, the shop served burgers, spaghetti, hot dogs and fried chicken. Those with a sweet tooth could purchase cookies and candy, and patrons could also purchase a watch, a necklace or jewelry at bargain prices. At the same location as the confectionery, Rose operated Rose's Tap Room, where the adult population was served for a few years. Rose had another adult establishment at 2804 R ½, the Gulf View Pavilion, managed by his son John Ned Rose Jr. Located near the Seawall, the tavern had a great view of the Gulf of Mexico.

Rose's Confectionary remained open until 1962. On April 29, 1967, Ned Rose passed away. His service was held at Holy Rosary Catholic Church under the direction of Strode-Armstrong Funeral Home. He was survived by his wife, Anna, two sons, John and Paul, and his daughter, Lillian Robinson. After his death. Anna Rose maintained ownership of the taproom and turned over operation of the business to her son John, who managed the bar until it closed in 1973. During Hurricane Ike, a national news cable service recorded John Ned Rose III walking down a flooded Galveston street with water over his knees. Rose survived the hurricane and continues to live in Galveston.

SHEPHERD'S CAFÉ

Originally located at 4023 Ball Street, Shepherd's Café was owned and operated by Ellis and Hattie Shepherd. The café opened in 1937 and remained open through the middle of the 1990s. An advertisement for the café in the *Galveston Examiner* on December 2, 1939, encouraged the community to come out and "Eat at one of the west end's best." It generated a loyal following and guaranteed a lunchtime crowd.

The initial location served customers through World War II before moving out in 1946. In 1947, the café relocated to 4101 Ball and made a few adjustments to accommodate its customer base. Around the same time the café moved, the spelling of the business name was altered slightly to Sheppard's Café before reverting to the original spelling. In 1954, the café moved again, to 4227 Sealy Street, where it stayed through the rest of the 1950s and into the 1960s.

The Shepherd family lived in the rear of the 4227 Sealy location, and one family member lived next door so they were always in proximity to the business. The family went through a transition in the late 1960s and early 1970s as Ellis and Hattie handed the day-to-day management to their son Ollie Shepherd. While Ollie ran the front of the house, his wife, Orelia, handled the back of the house and prepared all of the food.

Albert Dennis, a 1976 graduate of Ball High School, remembered comments made about the food and the menu and noted that the meal was worth the price of purchase and that portions were big enough to have leftovers the next day. Paul Frenchwood, a lifelong resident of Galveston, has fond memories of the café's menu of "soul food" and recalled that there was a different dinner special every day of the week. The pork chops, roast beef and fried chicken, along with gravy, two side dishes and a dessert of choice were sure to please.

In the later years of the café, a menu was not necessary. The locals knew what Shepherd's Café served each day of the week and that staff stayed pretty close to that script. The café remained open to the public well into the 1990s. Today, the location is an empty lot, but the memory of Shepherd's Café and the authentic soul food served by the Shepherd family from the corner of Forty-Third and Sealy remains.

SIMS ICE CREAM PARLOR

Will and Della Rivers Sims's Ice Cream Parlor was a child's paradise, where one could purchase a treat for a penny.

Will Sims was born in Willis, a city located eight miles north of Conroe, Texas. Della Rivers was born in Double Bayou, Texas, in a rural community located fifty miles southwest of Beaumont. It's unknown when or where Will and Della met, but the 1930 United States Census of Galveston recorded the married couple living at 2827 Avenue K and indicated they were married in 1929. The census also recorded Will's employment as a laborer on the Galveston wharf, while Della worked as a cook in a private home. In 1939, the Galveston City Directory noted that in addition to their jobs as a laborer and a domestic worker, Will and Della operated a soft-drink business at 1106 Twenty-Ninth Street.

By 1949, the couple had purchased a two-story building at 3001 Avenue M to serve as their home as well as a small grocery store. In 1952, the city directory noted 3001 Avenue M as both the Sims residence and the location of the newly named Sims Ice Cream Parlor.

The ice cream parlor was located in a family neighborhood and next door to West Point Baptist Church. It was in walking distance of the three African American public schools: Central High School, Booker T. Washington

The building that once housed Sims Ice Cream Parlor, located next door to West Point Baptist Church.

Elementary and George W. Carver Elementary. The African American Holy Rosary Catholic School was also located just a few blocks from the store, at Thirty-First and Avenue N.

While the store was advertised as an ice cream parlor, initially selling vanilla, strawberry and chocolate ice cream, other items could also be purchased. There were large jars of whole pickles, jars of cookies and boxes of assorted candy, soft drinks, bubble gum and regular gum. The ice cream was sold in a cone or in hand-packed pints, and the establishment was open seven days a week.

Clora Otems, born and raised in Galveston, recalled that when she was a child she purchased Dixie or Jack brand cookies for a penny and an ice cream cone for a nickel. One of her favorite treats was to purchase a pickle and a hard peppermint stick that was inserted into the pickle and used as a straw. The blended peppermint flavor and pickle juice was delicious, and once the juice was gone, she would eat what remained of the peppermint and the pickle. A lifelong member of West Point Baptist Church, Otems also recalled the adult members of the church reminding the youth not to spend their church money at the store.

As a child, Georgia Robbins lived across the street from the ice cream parlor. She, too, was a member of West Point Baptist Church. She and her four siblings stayed home alone while their mother and stepfather worked and were told never to leave the house. With such a large family, there was little money for treats such as candy and ice cream. Adults in the neighborhood would see them sitting on the front steps of their home while other children were playing in the streets. Some of the neighbors gave them a little change because they were so well behaved and always obeyed their parents. Robbins said they never told their parents, but they would leave the house and go to the ice cream parlor and purchase something. Robbins said she may have purchased a Jack cookie a few times, but her favorite treat was an ice cream cone and, if she had the money for it, a double-dip cone. The Robbins children would eat everything they purchased before their mother and stepfather returned home. She also recalled that on Sundays, just before Sunday school was dismissed, the youth were reminded that during the break between Sunday school and 11:00 a.m. service they were not to spend the money meant for church at the ice cream parlor!

A longtime Galvestonian, Gloria Ellisor recalled many Baptist district meetings held at West Point Baptist Church. During breaks, the attendees purchased ice cream and snacks from Sims Ice Cream Parlor. This writer recalls going with her father as a child to Sims to purchase one pint of hand-packed ice cream. We were a family of five, and all of us were given a serving of the ice cream. However, our mother seldom ate any.

Sims Ice Cream Parlor existed for more than 30 years. Few people knew Will, and most recalled that it was Della who managed the shop. After Will passed on May 21, 1957, Della managed the store until her health failed. She passed away on May 16, 1994, living to the age of 101. Today, West Point Baptist Church owns the building.

SQUARE DEAL CAFÉ

According to Galveston City Directories, in 1949, the Square Deal Café was owned and managed by Mattie Captain. It was originally located at 3328 Ball Street. In 1951, B.H. Humphrey was noted in the directories as the proprietor. The 1952 directory identified the Square Deal Service Station and Garage at the 3328 Ball location, under the management of Thomas Hickerson. By 1953, George and Pearl Dudley were the owners, and by the time the Dudleys acquired the café, it had moved to 3920 Ball. One Galveston City Directory advertisement noted that the café was open for breakfast, lunch and dinner from 7:00 a.m. every morning until midnight, seven days a week.

The Dudleys operated the Square Deal for more than fifteen years, and during that time, they became very involved with the city. George Dudley was born on September 4, 1896, in Angleton, Texas. Pearl was from New Iberia, Louisiana, where she was born in 1902. The Dudleys were members of the Mount Olive Baptist Church, and George volunteered annually for the World Service Day project sponsored by the Gibson Branch of the YMCA. He was a veteran of World War I and a member of the Greater Galveston Lodge Number 415. In 1967, Pearl passed away, followed by George's passing in 1968. After their deaths, Esther Hamilton assumed ownership and operation of the café. Ownership would transfer two more times, to Rose L. Virgil and Ms. Emma Adams, before Ivery Terry Sr. made arrangements to purchase the café in 1972.

Ivery Terry was born on March 10, 1905, in Opelousas, Louisiana, and was a resident of Galveston for twenty-eight years. He and his wife, Mary, had two sons, Ivery Jr. and Charles. According to his grandson Craig Bowie, Terry purchased the Square Deal when he got injured at work and wanted a job with less risk of injury. After he acquired the café, Terry started

The Square Deal Café. Date unknown. *University of North Texas Libraries, The Portal to Texas History, Texas Historical Commission.*

serving soul food to the lunch crowd. Soon, Mary added a breakfast menu to the offerings. Bowie mentioned that the Square Deal had daily soul food specials served at both lunch and dinner. One day, the main course would be oxtails with two sides, usually rice with gravy and beans, and the dessert would include a slice of pie or cake. The next day, it would be meatloaf, with the sides and dessert. Bowie remembered that the portions were always generous. His favorite meal was the steak with mashed potatoes and green beans. It was a meal his grandparents were happy to serve him, and he made sure he always cleaned his plate.

Regular customers to the café came from the cotton sheds and warehouses located within walking distance. Many men were employed in the area at that time, and when the different sheds or warehouses stayed open twenty-four hours to accommodate the workload, the Square Deal followed suit in order to accommodate the workers' schedules.

A fire in the residence above the café in 1972 affected the establishment when 230,000 gallons of water used to put out the fire caused approximately $3,500 of damage to the building. Despite the challenge, the Square Deal was repaired and reopened. Terry passed away in 1974, and the Terry family maintained ownership of the café until 1976, when they passed the keys to Joe Frager. He retained ownership until 1981, when Tyrone Frazier took over the establishment. He and Kodel Frazier managed the café until 1985, when the doors closed a final time, ending more than forty years of service to the community.

TEMPLE'S CAFÉ

Temple's Café was a place to get good home-style meals on Sunday and a soulful lunch during the week. It was a labor of love for the entire Temple family. Located at 2702 Church Street, Temple's Café was owned and operated by John Sullivan and Zola Temple. The Temples started their culinary career at the Old Blimp Base and Naval Air Station (NAS) in Hitchcock, Texas, that operated during 1943–44. After they left the Blimp Base, the Temples worked in Galveston for the Paddio family, who owned and operated Pearl's Café, located around the corner from Gus Allen's Café. When Gus Allen closed his café, John and Zola leased the building from Allen and opened their own restaurant, Temple's Café.

John Temple was born in Blessing, Texas, and Zola was from Orange, Texas, but the couple called Galveston home. On the island, their household eventually grew to include eight children. As their family grew, so did their family-owned and -operated business. Growing up, all of the children worked in the café until they were either drafted into the service or went to college. In the summer months when school was out, nieces and nephews helped out. The Temples delivered lunch all over Galveston to businesses both north and south of Broadway and to nearby beauty parlors and barbershops. Lunch was the big seller during the week, but the café's most popular day was Sunday, when customers packed the café for pork roast and dressing, the Temples' specialty, along with stuffed bell peppers, another crowd favorite.

John Temple died on April 17, 1956, at the age of fifty-three. His son Pastor Jerry Temple remembered that his dad loved the Budweiser Clydesdales. The Clydesdales came to Galveston once a year, and John Temple never missed seeing them. A prized photograph of him sitting on one of the horses hung in a place of honor at the café, proudly placed for all of the patrons to see.

After John died, Zola continued to operate the café with the help of her sons. Her grandchildren worked at the café on weekends, delivered phone orders and handled the ice cream parlor. Zola's granddaughter Lucy Smith Taylor recalled how she loved to work weekends for her grandmother. She always knew she would work in the ice cream parlor and could eat all the strawberry ice cream she wanted. She noted that her grandmother's strawberry ice cream was the best, while Jerry Temple championed her lemon ice cream.

In September 1961, Hurricane Carla made landfall on the Texas coast as a Category 4 hurricane. Tornadoes spawned by the hurricane destroyed several buildings in Galveston, including the building that housed Temple's Cafe. After Hurricane Carla, the café never reopened, and Zola Temple went to work for American National Insurance Company in the company's dining room, where she worked until she retired. On August 5, 2007, Zola Temple died at the age of ninety-three years old.

THE PEOPLE'S CAFÉ

The People's Café, located at 411 Twenty-Fifth Street, was owned and operated by Louisiana native and World War I veteran James Hudson. A café by the same name operated at 213 Twentieth Street until approximately 1926. However, there was a connection between the two cafés other than in name.

A 1933 advertisement for the People's Cafe in the *Galveston Sentinel* promoted "good things to eat, regular meals, short order meals and special breakfast plates." A notice in the classified section of the *Sentinel* in April 1934 noted a name change to People's Café and Beer Garden. The café also offered a private buffet service, special rates for group parties, music and ice-cold beer on tap at all hours.

When World War II broke out, the People's Café partnered with the City of Galveston to provide breakfasts for the local African American enlistees leaving for boot camp. The country was preparing for war, and as young men enlisted around the area, the Galveston Draft Board hosted a ceremonial sendoff for the future troops. For the Black soldiers, that included a delicious breakfast at the People's Café; the White enlistees ate at the Island Café. On November 20, 1940, ten young African American men ate a 6:00 a.m. breakfast at the People's Café before they boarded the Texas Bus Lines for a

The old location of the People's Café, at 411 Twenty-Fifth Street, as seen today.

trip to Houston. Galveston mayor Brantly Harris Sr. made a few comments, and the Ball High School band played a few numbers prior to the bus's departure. The Ball High ROTC also attended the special event.

By 1941, James's wife, Olivia, had joined her husband to help run the café, which added homemade pastries to its menu. The café also served delicious sandwiches and soft drinks and provided great music. James Hudson passed away on December 10, 1941, at the U.S. Marine Hospital in Galveston. He was laid to rest at Galveston Municipal Cemetery. The People's Café shut down after Hudson passed. Willie and Pearl Anderson took over the space and opened Island City Café, which they operated until 1952, when the location welcomed Wyatt Seafood Restaurant to the building, operated by H.W. Wyatt. By 1955, the building was vacant and would remain unoccupied into the early 1970s. In 1972, the La Fitte Club opened at the location, and other types of business followed.

The People's Café made a significant contribution to the lives of those who grew up in Galveston, especially those who served in the armed forces during World War II. James and Olivia Hudson will always be remembered as willing to step forward and serve the community. Their work will never be forgotten.

TIP TOP CAFÉ

The Tip Top Café was more than a restaurant offering delicious food; it was also the hub for those who wanted to stay informed on events or news relevant to the African American community and Galveston. The café's owner, Courtney Bernard Murray, was born in Grand Cane, Louisiana, in 1902. Grand Cane is a small village located in the Shreveport–Bossier City metropolitan area. Courtney's parents, Judge and Tempie Murray, moved to Galveston in search of better employment opportunities when Courtney was three years old. In 1910, the United States Census recorded the family residence at 3009 Avenue L .When Courtney was seven years old, his father secured a job on the Galveston docks. By the time the 1920 census was taken, seventeen-year-old Courtney had entered the workforce, employed as a driver for a clothing store.

Courtney married Sadie Jackson of Wharton, Texas. It is unknown exactly when they met or married, but the 1935 birth certificate of their first child, Courtney Jr., noted the married couple residing in Wharton. At the time, Courtney was employed as a salesman and Sadie was employed as a housekeeper. The household included Sadie's three children from a previous marriage, Rufus, Jennie and Stella. Their second child, Delores, was born in Galveston in 1936.

Sometime around 1939, Courtney purchased property at 2627 Avenue F and opened the Tip Top Café as a twenty-four-hour restaurant. Not a

Courtney B. Murray with his daughters Jessie and Delores and family friend Miss Eddie inside of his establishment, the Tip Top Café. *Courtesy Murray family.*

trained cook and with little experience in the restaurant business, he hired a full-time staff to manage the day-to-day operations. His role was manager, bookkeeper and official greeter. The menu was extensive, recalled Lettie Holden, Sadie and Courtney's granddaughter. She worked at the café during her teens in the 1960s and remembered that the menu included chili, beef stew, rice, black-eyed peas, greens, fried fish, fried chicken, pork chops, cornbread, hamburgers, biscuits and much more. She remembered a dessert selection of homemade bread pudding, peach cobbler and several cakes offered daily. Very often, specialty items were added to the menu for a limited time. Beverages included coffee, tea, sodas and beer. Breakfast was available all day and was a popular draw with the customer base, some of whom worked odd hours at the port. Tommie McNeil, who lived near the café in his youth, recalled having breakfast at the café. The scrambled eggs were better than his mom's, he recollected, "all yellow, fluffy and well-seasoned." In the 1940s, an entire meal could be purchased for one dollar to three dollars, depending on what was ordered. A 1939 ad in the *Galveston Daily News* indicated that the café also delivered. On weekend nights, Courtney brought in a band to entertain the clientele.

Courtney treated his staff well and took a personal interest in each of them. Odessa Phillips, Mrs. Paris at the time, worked at the café in the

1950s and was a waitress who occasionally covered the Tap Room, a room separated from the restaurant where alcoholic beverages were sold. The Tap Room had pinball machines and, years earlier, slot machines, commonly referred to as "one-armed bandits." She worked in other capacities and was willing to do whatever was needed to keep the business productive. She recalled that Courtney once offered her and other staff an opportunity to attend business school, which she accepted. After she graduated from O.E. Brown School of Business in Galveston, she moved to Hitchcock, Texas, and opened her own restaurant. She later stated, "Mr. Murray and his wife were very generous to me."

The Tip Top Café became a well-known restaurant and popular hangout, but Courtney wore many other hats. His granddaughter Sarae Rex (Toni) recalled being told that her grandfather once owned a pig farm in Hitchcock. However, being a city boy, she added that the venture didn't last long. He was also very active in the community and used the café as a point of contact. He was a member of the Galveston Negro Chamber of Commerce, supported the Gibson Branch of the YMCA, was the owner of the local Buccaneers baseball and football teams and supported several nonprofit service organizations. At the café, tickets were sold for various events held in Galveston, including those held at Galveston's City Auditorium. He also sold tickets to all Central High School sports events as well as any fundraising event for local organizations. The Tip Top was also a City of Galveston Poll Tax station. Payment of a poll tax was a prerequisite to vote or register to vote for a number of states until 1966. Implemented during the Jim Crow era, the tax of between $1.00 and $1.50 was an expense most African Americans could not afford and was an attempt to keep them from exercising their right to vote. Courtney volunteered as a Galveston County voter registrar deputy and several nights a week was available until midnight to accept poll tax payments and/or register citizens so they would be eligible to vote. During World War II, Courtney provided free entertainment for the soldiers stationed at Camp Wallace in Galveston and discounted meals if they visited the café.

Courtney was also a promoter who brought the top African American talent of the 1940s, '50s and '60s to Galveston's City Auditorium. Because of his efforts, Galvestonians had an opportunity to see Louis Jordan, Billy Eckstein, Sara Vaughn, Joe Turner, Peg Leg Bates, Bill "Bojangles" Robinson, Count Basie, Cab Calloway and His Cotton Club Orchestra, Lionel Hampton and His Orchestra, Charles Brown, Earl "Father" Hines, Victor Hugo Greene, Roy Milton and His Soul Senders, Duke Ellington,

Nat King Cole and the international all-girl orchestra the Sweethearts of Rhythm, to name a few. The archives of the *Galveston Daily News* reveal that Courtney had a well-known artist in Galveston at least two or three times a month; some of them returned multiple times. In the 1940s, tickets to Courtney's shows cost between $0.80 and $1.00 and increased to $2.00 over a twenty-year span. Tickets could be purchased at the Tip Top Café, the City Auditorium and a few other select businesses. On all of his advertisements, Courtney included the following statement, "Section Reserved for Whites," as promoters who brought White talent to Galveston had a similar statement on their ads for "Negroes." After the shows, the artists would dine at the Tip Top Café. Odessa Phillips recalled serving many of the entertainers during her time of employment, including Etta James. Often, with celebrities in the café, the dining and fun lasted until sunup the next morning.

The Tip Top Café closed in the late 1960s, when the City of Galveston implemented eminent domain on Courtney's property and the property that surrounded his. Though he was compensated, his granddaughter Sarae Rex stated that he didn't want to start all over again. Though he no longer had the café and had stopped bringing entertainers in for the community, he remained active. He served on many committees and continued to support nonprofit service organizations. He was also able to devote more time to his church, the historic Avenue L Baptist Church, where he served as deacon and chaired the finance committee. He also served as an alternate election judge for many years and volunteered for the census counts and always made himself available to speak with groups concerned with local, state and national issues.

Over the years, Courtney received many awards for his service to the community. At age eighty-two, he took a part-time job with the Job Corps at the Texas Employment Commission. The program offered vocational training for young people ages eighteen to twenty-two. When asked why he was still working, he replied, "I just like helping young people." On November 23, 1988, Courtney was presented with a humanitarian award from Texas governor William P. Clements Jr. for his accomplishments, general contributions to the community and support of the military. The award cites his work in the Job Corps program and recognizes his contributions during World War II. Courtney Bernard Murray Sr. passed away on May 26, 2001, at the age of ninety-nine.

Jack Strange's Confectionery / Quality Café

Nine different food establishments occupied the building at 1114 Twenty-Ninth Street over the course of thirty years. Each made a contribution to the community, and memories of many of them live on. The history of the long succession of cafés and grills began in the middle of the 1940s, right around the end of World War II, when Jack Strange opened a confectionery at 1114 Twenty-Ninth Street. Born in Crockett, Texas, on September 7, 1905, Strange operated the confectionery for a few years before his wife, Izetta, changed the format and renamed the establishment Quality Café. In 1952, Meredith and Lucille Sanford took over the business. They changed the name to C&L Waffle Shop and altered the menu to reflect the new name. The waffle shop enjoyed modest success until Meredith Sanford passed away in 1956.

After Sanford's death, Gladys Thibodeaux took over the location and opened Gladys's Kitchen. After her death in 1958, Wilbur Henderson claimed the spot and relocated his café, the L&M, from 1314 Twenty-Ninth Street. The L&M Café was open seven days a week and specialized in fine foods and home-cooked meals. The L&M operated until 1962, when Roxie Taylor took over and opened the Twenty-Ninth Street Grill.

In 1964, Odessa Lister opened the Gay Pree Café after the Twenty-Ninth Street Grill closed. She operated the café for four years until Jack Strange stepped back in, changed the name to Gay Paree Café and took over management until 1970, when Strange passed the keys to Willie Winston. Winston changed the name yet again, to the Serina Café. The Serina was short-lived, and soon, Claude Merchant had his eye on the spot. Merchant opened the Twenty-Ninth Street Café in 1971, which began the final installment of eating establishments at 1114 Twenty-Ninth Street. Merchant would boast the longest consecutive years of service to the public before he closed his café in 1979. Merchant was born in 1910 in Cedar Lane, Texas, and was the ninth of eighteen children. Before he opened the Twenty-Ninth Street Café, he served as chef at the Crystal Palace Restaurant in the historic Crystal Palace Bathhouse, once located on Seawall Boulevard at Twenty-Fourth Street. Merchant passed away at John Sealy Hospital on June 23, 1997.

Chapter 5

Gone but Not Forgotten

Short Orders and Depression-Era Cafés

Some of the memories of Galveston's African American–owned eating establishments have almost passed into history. Long before franchised restaurants were commonplace, and deep in the middle of the Jim Crow South, many African American family-owned businesses served the citizens of Galveston. A few of these establishments operated for just a brief period, often appearing only once in the Galveston City Directories. Many of these opened during the Great Depression of the 1930s, when the economic situation of African Americans worsened as their labor force suffered two to three times the unemployment rate of their White counterparts. It was against these overwhelming odds that African American citizens of Galveston undertook the courageous risk of opening eating establishments. The following are just a few of their stories.

WYATT'S SEAFOOD

One such restaurant was owned by Henry W. Wyatt. Wyatt was born in Hempstead, Texas, on June 15, 1886. He moved to Galveston around 1914 and spent the rest of his life on the island. In 1929, Wyatt opened a restaurant at 2611 Market Street. He moved the business to 2804 Avenue R ½ in 1931 and named the new location Gulf View Dining

Room. The restaurant went through several more name changes over the years, including Wyatt Seafood Shop and Henry W. Wyatt Seafood, before he finally settled on Wyatt's Seafood. Along with the name changes, the location shifted around on the 2800 block of Avenue R ½ before it settled at 2812 R ½. It remained on Avenue R ½ until 1952, when Wyatt relocated the business to 411 Twenty-Fifth Street, where it remained until the restaurant closed in 1954 after more than twenty-five years of service to the community. Wyatt passed away at his residence on October 6, 1965. During his fifty-one-year residency, he was an active member of Progressive Baptist Church. He was interred at Galveston's Memorial Cemetery under the direction of Fields Funeral Home. There was no mention in his obituary of surviving children.

WEST END SANDWICH SHOP

The West End Sandwich Shop operated at 4305 Ball Street. Robert J. Morant, the proprietor, served the citizens of Galveston for a span of a few years in the mid-1930s. Morant was born in Galveston on December 1, 1912, and attended the Galveston public schools. After he graduated from Central High School, he attended Wiley College, where he was a member of Phi Beta Sigma fraternity. Morant was a member of the congregation of Hunter's Chapel CME Church and served on its trustee and stewardship committees. After he retired from Sears Roebuck Company, Morant went to work for Thomas D. Armstrong at Strode Armstrong Mortuary. Morant died at his residence in La Marque on December 7, 1976. He was survived by his wife, Ernestine Banks, son James Otis Johnson Jr. and daughter Charlotte Marie Caligone. Morant is buried at Rising Star Cemetery in La Marque, Texas.

ISLAND CITY CAFÉ

Louisiana natives Willie and Pearl Anderson opened the Island City Café at 419 Twenty-Fifth Street in the 1930s. Willie Anderson was born in New Iberia on December 8, 1899, and Pearl was born in Bunkie on July 15, 1903. Soon after the couple opened their café, they relocated the business to

411 Twenty-Fifth Street, into space previously occupied by James Hudson's People's Café. Willie and Pearl operated the restaurant from that location until they closed the business in 1952. Willie died in Galveston on June 14, 1958, followed by Pearl's death in 1971. They are buried at Galveston's Memorial Cemetery.

2827 MARKET

In 1929, Nathan and Willie Jolivet opened a restaurant at 2827 Market Street on the corner of Market and Twenty-Ninth Streets. They maintained their business at that location until 1937. Nathan Jolivet was from Baldwin, Louisiana, and his wife, Willie, was born in Brazos County, Texas. After they closed their restaurant, Ruby Lucas opened the Twin Sisters Café in 1938. In 1939, Willie Robinson took over the location and opened Robinson's Café. By 1941, the building was vacant.

PRESS ADDISON

In 1930, Press Addison opened a restaurant at 118 Sixteenth Street. Never known by any other name than Addison's, the business was strategically placed to take advantage of the dockworkers along the wharf and those employed at the massive Fourteenth Street grain elevator. Addison's location was one of the very few African American businesses located east of Twenty-Fifth Street in Galveston. The restaurant closed in 1935.

WALKER'S CAFÉ

Lucille Walker opened up a small café at 718 Fortieth Street in 1930. By 1935, she had relocated across the street to 4001 Ball Street and named the restaurant Walker's Café. In 1937, she closed the business.

ETTA DICKENS

In the early 1930s, Etta Dickens started serving food from a storefront at 5328 Ball Street. Located in the westernmost section of the factory district, Dickens' Café was in proximity to the majority of the cotton compresses and warehouses concentrated on the north side of Broadway Boulevard. In addition to the restaurant, Dickens rented out furnished rooms in her residence at 714 Twenty-Fifth Street. By the middle of the decade, the eating establishment had closed, but Dickens continued to rent furnished rooms at her home.

RANDLE BROTHERS CAFÉ

The Randle Brothers Café was open for a very short period in the late 1930s and early 1940s. It was located at 2902 Sealy. The owner was Daniel Randle.

DURGON'S CAFÉ

Durgon's Café was located at 2627 Mechanic Street. It opened in the late 1930s and remained open for a few years before it closed in 1942. Emile Durgon was the owner.

5221 AVENUE M

In the late 1930s, Napoleon Edwards opened a restaurant at 5221 Avenue M. Edward's venture lasted about a year. Mary Byrd opened a soft-drink fountain from the location after Edwards closed his restaurant. Byrd's fountain had a short lifespan as well, and by 1941, the location was a grocery store.

Restaurants located near the port capitalized on the workforce, many of whom were African American men, as seen here hauling cotton along a pier in 1925.

2712 MARKET

The storefront located at 2712 Market Street hosted a number of food establishments in the 1930s and 1940s, a few of which were open for more than one year. Among them was William Johnson's Longshoremen's Café, opened in 1938. A year later, Roger's Progressive Club Restaurant opened, owned and operated by Howard Newton. The Progressive closed in 1940, and Sylvia Hays Restaurant opened and stayed in business until 1942. Like the others who preceded her at this location, Hays relied on the dockworkers as lunch customers.

Avenue M Lunch Room

In the middle of the 1930s, Marion Henry opened the Avenue M Lunch Room at 3001 Avenue M. Located next door to West Point Baptist Church, Henry's lunchroom had a great location. His wife, Lucille, worked with him at the restaurant. Together, the couple successfully ran the lunchroom until 1942. The location later served the public as Sims Ice Cream Parlor. The building is owned today by West Point Baptist Church. According to Reverend Kevin Tillmon, a 1975 graduate of Galveston Ball High School and current minister of Christian education at West Point Baptist Church, the building is a safe haven and used for activities related to youth ministry and Vacation Bible Schools.

Isaiah Brown

In proximity to West Point Baptist Church, Isaiah Brown opened his restaurant at 3027 Avenue M. Brown's restaurant operated without an official name from the early 1930s until it closed in 1942. Brown was born in 1888 in Brazoria, Texas, and lived in Galveston for more than fifty years. He died on the island in 1967 and was buried at Galveston's Memorial Cemetery.

Williams Café

Edward "E.C." Williams opened his café at 2705 Market Street in the early 1930s. Within a few years, he moved the business one block east, to 2626 Market. Without an official name, locals dubbed the establishment "Williams Café." It closed in the early 1940s after almost a decade of service. E.C. Williams was a retired longshoreman who was born in 1887 in Morgan City, Louisiana. He was a longtime resident of Galveston and devoted member of Mount Olive Baptist Church. Williams passed away in Galveston on July 2, 1970. He was preceded in death by his wife, Matilda, and survived by a daughter and a sister. He is interred at Galveston's Memorial Cemetery.

COZY CABIN CAFÉ

The Cozy Cabin was a café located at 3427 Church Street. It was owned and operated by Eli Johnson. The café was open for a short time in the late 1930s.

GREENE & DILLS CAFÉ

Greene & Dills Café was located at 2525 Market. It was operated by Louis Greene and Rebecca Dill. The café was open for a short span in the middle of the 1930s.

MISSISSIPPI INN RESTAURANT

The Mississippi Inn Restaurant was open for a short time in the late 1930s and early 1940s and was located at 2705 Postoffice Street. The Galveston City Directed noted William Allen as the business owner in 1939. The 1941 directory was the last one to include the business. That year, Julia Rowen was noted as the owner and operator.

HENRY DAVIS

Henry Davis operated a restaurant at 2423 Water Street (Harborside Drive). Davis opened the restaurant in the middle of the 1930s and closed it in 1940. His restaurant was another establishment that catered to the workforce of the nearby wharves. By 1943, the business was gone.

RISING STAR CAFÉ

The Rising Star Café served meals for a few short years between 1944 and 1948. It was owned and operated by William Thomas and listed in the 1947

African American stevedores wait to service a ship docked at Pier 39 in 1926.

Galveston City Directory as the William Thomas Restaurant, located at 702 Thirty-Seventh Street. In 1949, O.T. Wheeler took over the location and changed the name of the business to Thirty-Third Street Grill.

THE PARAMOUNT CAFÉ

The Paramount Café opened in the middle of the 1940s. Luke E. Wyles Sr. owned and operated the restaurant, located at 2812 Postoffice Street. The Paramount served the community for several years before it closed in the 1950s. Wyles was born on June 5, 1905, in Alexandria, Louisiana, and later attended the Tuskegee Institute. After he arrived in Galveston, Wyles was an active member of Mount Olive Baptist Church, where he served on the board of trustees and taught Sunday school. He passed away on January 30, 1999, and was interred at Galveston's Memorial Cemetery. He was preceded in death by his parents, wife Earnye Mae and his only son, Luke E. Wyles Jr.

BLACK CAT CAFÉ / BLACK CAT TAVERN

The Black Cat was a popular name in Galveston in the early 1940s. The Black Cat Café, located at 3501 Ball Street, opened in 1940 and closed in 1946. Robert Wright was the proprietor. Robert Evans owned the Black Cat Tavern, located at 413 Twenty-Fifth Street. The tavern opened in 1942 and closed in 1946. An advertisement in the 1945–46 Galveston City Directory noted that the tavern served good food, beer and wine. The directory also noted that, in addition to the tavern, Evans owned the Black Cat Taxi Service at 2713 Church Street.

KELTON SAMS' RESTAURANT

For a few years during the middle of the 1940s, Letha Sams operated Kelton Sams' Restaurant at 713 Forty-Third Street. Kelton Sams Jr. remembers his mom being a great cook, with her specialties based on Creole and Cajun recipes, which she prepared lovingly for the men working on the wharves.

3927 BALL STREET

Ernest S. Walker managed multiple businesses from his location at 3927 Ball Street. In 1947, the city directory noted that Walker sold alcoholic beverages and operated an automobile garage from the address. In 1949, Walker transformed his corner at Ball and Fortieth Streets again and opened the Fortieth Street Grill. The grill closed in 1956.

THE GREEN PARROT CAFÉ

The Green Parrot Café opened in the early 1940s at 712 Twenty-Sixth Street. The building also offered furnished rooms for rent. Meals may have been offered as part of room and board. A.L. Reed and Lewis Simpson were listed as the proprietors. By 1948, the business was gone.

THE BLUE ROOM INN RESTAURANT

The Blue Room Inn Restaurant was located at 2728 Church Street, on the corner of Twenty-Ninth Street. The business opened in 1942 and closed within a few years. City directories noted Gertie Payne as the operator. The business preceded one of the most well-known African American–owned restaurants in the history of Galveston, Honey Brown's, opened by Nelson "Honey" Brown after the Blue Room Inn closed.

LEE'S CAFÉ

Lee's Café opened in the early 1940s. Located at 3702 Winnie Street, the café was also often referred to as Lee's Place. Lettie Fred was the proprietor when it opened. Fred was born on August 6, 1896, in Willis, Texas. In 1946, she passed the day-to-day management of the café to Lee and Lillian Campbell, who expanded the café's menu to include alcoholic beverages. Lee's Café remained in operation until 1955. Fred passed away at the University of Texas Medical Branch in Galveston on June 23, 1965, and was laid to rest at Galveston's Memorial Cemetery.

GRAND TELL GROCERY & CAFÉ

Drummie Smith was born in Eagle Lake, Texas, on December 28, 1908, and was a resident of Galveston for over forty years. Around 1944, Drummie opened the Grand Tell Grocery & Café at 2727 Winnie Street. In the early 1950s, the establishment moved around the corner, to 704 Twenty-Eighth Street. Ressie Johnson was listed as the owner for a few years before the establishment reverted back to Drummie. Soon after, Drummie dropped the word "café" from the business and rebranded it as the Grand Tell Grocery. For thirty-two years, Drummie operated the retail grocery and worked as the in-house butcher. On April 10, 1961, Drummie passed away at UTMB in Galveston. During his life, Smith was a member of Mount Olive Baptist Church. His funeral arrangements were made by Fields Funeral Home followed by burial at Galveston's Memorial Cemetery. After his death, the grocery continued to operate at the same location with his wife, Lela, in charge of the operation. She maintained ownership of the grocery store until 1968, after which Albert Barbie took over the location and named the business after himself. Barbie's remained open until the early 1970s. In 1972, the Galveston City Directory noted that the location was vacant.

POWELL'S CAFÉ

Powell's Café opened at 2603 Market Street in the early 1940s under the ownership of Felix and Roberta Powell. By 1949, the café had moved a block east to 2517 Market. In 1953, the Galveston City Directory noted Thelma Powell as owner. In 1955, after she remarried, Mrs. Stanford, as she was known to her customers, moved the establishment next door to 2515 Market. Stanford closed Powell's Café around 1960. Galveston directories noted the space as vacant until 1962, when Mama's Diner opened at the address. The proprietor of Mama's Diner was noted in the city directory as Corelia Daggs. The diner's specialty was seafood dinners. Mama's Diner remained in operation until 1966. In 1967, Country Kitchen Restaurant opened in the space and remained there until it closed in the early 1970s. Galveston City Directories noted Cora Virgil as the owner.

3626–28 CHURCH STREET

The building located at 3628 Church Street has hosted a number of business establishments since 1921. After the Oleander Café moved away from the building in the late 1940s and relocated to Thirty-Seventh Street, the Key Hole Café opened for business in 1949. In continual operation, the restaurant's name changed multiple times and was known over the years as Eli's Café, El's Café, Utopia Café and, finally, in 1961, the Sky Rocket Café. The second storefront in the building, 3626 Church Street, was the location of Tillman's Sandwich Shop, owned and operated by Thomas Tillman. Tillman's Sandwich Shop opened in 1960 and operated for a few years before Cora's Sandwich Shop replaced it in 1967. In 1969, the Key Hole Café was resurrected at the address. During the early 1970s, Galveston City Directories noted the building vacant again, but by 1975, the Key Hole Café was reopened. The café closed for a final time in 1983. As the owner of multiple businesses at the location, Thomas Tillman spent a lot of time in the building. Tillman was born on March 28, 1901, in Jeanerette, Louisiana. He was a veteran of the U.S. Army and a member of International Longshoremen's Association Local 1453. In addition to his businesses on Twenty-Fifth Street, Tillman operated Tillman's Café on the corner of Thirty-Seventh and Church for many years. Tillman passed away on February 16, 1983. His service was held at Greater Saint Matthews Baptist Church, where he was a member, followed by burial at Mainland Cemetery in Hitchcock, Texas.

EL MOROCCO INN & DINING ROOM

In the late 1940s, Georgia Shanks opened a beauty shop within her spacious two-story house at 3311 Ball Street. In addition to the beauty shop, Shanks operated a boardinghouse from the address. Several years later, Shanks added a third business within her home when she opened the El Morocco Inn & Dining Room. By 1954, her dining room was known simply as the El Morocco Inn. The restaurant closed in 1964 after Shanks suffered a stroke and moved to San Antonio to live with her sister. She died there on August 6, 1964. She is interred at Hillside Cemetery in Cuero, Texas.

A.V.'S CAFÉ

Ada Evans opened A.V.'s Café at 2622 Winnie Street in the late 1940s and operated the café continually until 1960. During the café's years of operation, Evans shared her space with several other African American businesses, including the IXL Laundry, the Louisiana Drug Store and B&B's Beauty Shop. After A.V.'s Café closed in 1960, various restaurants occupied the building before it was demolished in the 1970s.

BOWMAN'S CAFÉ

Bowman's Café opened at 2820 Avenue R ½ at the end of World War II. The café was owned and operated by Arthur Bowman. His wife, Audrey, helped at the restaurant and also worked as a dispatcher for IXL Taxi Cab Service. The café remained open throughout the 1940s. After it closed, Bowman's culinary skills kept him employed at the Seaview Café and later as a chef for the Gulf Colorado & Santa Fe Railroad (GC&SF). The Jambalaya Café replaced Bowman's Café and occupied the building for more than thirty years.

CITY CAFÉ

The City Café opened at 512 Twenty-Ninth Street in 1944. Rosie Collins owned and operated the café. The restaurant catered to the expanding workforce that arrived in the city after the end of World War II. The café remained open until 1952.

DEFENSE CAFÉ / NEW DEAL CAFÉ

The Defense Café also opened in the mid-1940s. The café originally opened at 2615 Market Street, but by 1947, it had relocated to 613 Twenty-Eighth Street. Bertha Conway operated the business until 1949, when Archie Hicks took over management and changed the name to New Deal Cafe. Within a couple of years, the business was gone.

LADY LUCK CAFÉ

In 1944, Samuel Washington opened the Lady Luck Café at 702 Thirty-Seventh Street. He remained open for a few years but by 1949 had transferred ownership to Edward Davis, who changed the business name to the Hi Hat Inn. Davis closed the Hi Hat in the early 1950s.

MITCHELL'S CAFÉ

A 1949 Galveston City Directory advertisement for Mitchell Thibodeaux's café, where honey fried chicken was a house specialty.

Mitchell's Café opened at 417 Twenty-Fifth Street in 1944. Mitchell Thibodeaux was the owner and operator. During the café's short existence, Thibodeaux changed the name of the business to Mitchell's Supper Club before he changed it a final time to Mitchell's. Thibodeaux was born on September 17, 1890, in Opelousas, Louisiana, and was a World War I veteran. He passed away in Houston, Texas, on March 21, 1965. He is buried at Barber's Chapel Cemetery in Hitchcock, Texas. After Thibodeaux closed his café in the early 1950s, John W. McGaffey opened the Ambassador Café at the location.

PETE'S CAFÉ

Pete's Café opened for business during a very active period in the middle of the 1940s. Peter Williams was the owner of the establishment located on the corner of Ball and Twenty-Ninth Streets, at 2827–29 Ball Street. In addition to food, Williams sold cold beer. The café closed in the early 1950s.

ROSENBERG HAMBURGER STAND

During the 1940s, Theo Preston and Edward H. Huff opened the Rosenberg Hamburger Stand at 317 Twenty-Fifth Street. The pair remained in business until 1948. After the hamburger stand closed, Paul Love took over the location and opened Loves Luncheonette. The luncheonette remained there for just a short time before it closed in 1952.

THE BIG APPLE RESTAURANT

The Big Apple Restaurant was located at 2708 Market Street and operated by Rosie Arsberry. The restaurant opened in 1944. By the early 1950s, the business was gone.

SODA'S PLACE RESTAURANT

Richard and Alma Simmons opened Soda's Place Restaurant in 1941 at 2702 Market Street. The restaurant catered to the African American workforce until 1950. By 1952, the restaurant was gone and the location was occupied by Misse's Tavern.

THE BLUE FRONT CAFÉ

The Blue Front Café opened in 1940 at 717 Twenty-Ninth Street. William Robinson was the owner and operator. Before the Blue Front opened, the location had been used as an International Longshoremen's Association Hall and briefly as Paran's Grill in 1939. The Blue Front remained open through the 1940s; by 1949, Angie Robinson was listed as the café's owner in city directories. The Blue Front served its loyal customer base for over a decade before closing in the early 1950s.

3818 BALL STREET

The location at 3818 Ball Street hosted a revolving door of businesses between the middle of the 1940s through the middle of the 1950s. In 1944, it was known as the Westside Garage. By 1948, the Spotlight Grill opened, operated by Willie Murphy. Both businesses operated from the location for several years. In 1953, Frank Dennison assumed operation of the grill. By 1954, both the grill and the garage had been replaced by the Spotlite Tavern, also owned by Dennison.

PEARL CAFÉ

The Pearl Café was open briefly in 1948–49. The café was operated by Joseph W. Paddio. Born on October 26, 1901, in Opelousas, Louisiana, Paddio was a citizen of Galveston for sixty-five years and an active member of Mount Pilgrim Baptist Church. He passed away on November 11, 1981, and was interred at Lakeview Cemetery in Galveston. He was survived by his wife, Pearl, three sisters and one brother.

SILVER MOON CAFÉ

The Silver Moon Café opened in 1948 at 2804 Church Street and moved across the street to 2801 Church when the Pearl Café closed in late 1949. Robert Stevens managed the café, which closed in 1953.

SAM'S CAFÉ

Sam's Café opened at 2802 Church Street in 1942 and remained open until 1948. Galveston City Directories noted Sam L. Brown as the owner of the establishment. Brown was born in Georgia on April 30, 1894, and was a U.S. Army veteran of World War I. He passed away on May 20, 1976, in Texas City and was interred at Rising Star Cemetery in La Marque, Texas.

G&G LUNCH ROOM

In 1949, the G&G Lunch Room opened at 2802 Church Street. The Lunch Room was managed by Geneva Showers Davis. Davis operated the G&G until it closed in 1955. Davis was born in Galveston on March 6, 1906, and was a member of First Union Baptist Church. She died on January 18, 1970, and was interred at Mainland Memorial Cemetery in Hitchcock, Texas.

WHITE KITCHEN RESTAURANT

Clarence Williams was born in Lake Charles, Louisiana, on September 13, 1909. In 1953, he opened the White Kitchen Restaurant at 2820 Avenue R½. The *Galveston Daily News* recognized the restaurant in 1955 for its donation to the United Fund of Galveston. Williams's White Kitchen Restaurant was open for about twelve years before it closed after his death in 1965. A memorial service was held for Williams at the Taylor Funeral Home in La Marque. He was buried at the community's Rising Star Cemetery. He was survived by his wife, daughter and brother.

PEACHES CAFÉ

In 1954, Armond W "Peaches" Hurd Sr. opened Peaches Café at 2827 Ball Street. Hurd maintained the thriving business and in 1966 expanded the establishment to include pool tables. The café was known for its southern fried chicken, pork chops smothered in gravy and abundance of delicious vegetables. Peaches Café closed in the early 1970s. In addition to the café, Hurd operated the Gulf View Pavilion for a short time in the early 1960s. Hurd was born on June 13, 1910, in Rusk County, Texas. He was a veteran of World War II and a member of ILA Local 872 of Houston. Hurd passed away on February 21, 1971. He was survived by his wife, Mamie, as well as sons Armond Hurd Jr. and Carl Russell Hurd and daughters Cynthia Ann, Doris Marie and Darlene Louise. He is buried at Galveston's Memorial Cemetery.

SHOW PLACE GRILL

The Show Place Grill opened in the middle of the 1950s at 2701 Market Street. It was owned and operated by Anthony and Rosalie Taylor. The Taylors operated the grill during the 1960s but in 1971 closed for a brief period. When they reopened the Show Place Grill in 1973, they added alcoholic beverages to the menu. In 1984, the Show Place Grill closed. The building is currently occupied by a craft cocktail lounge.

WELCOME INN RESTAURANT / TRUE FRIEND GRILL

In the late 1950s, Lee and Ruby Franklin opened the Welcome Inn Restaurant at 2727 Market Street. In 1967, ownership of the restaurant transferred to Alexander Brown. Brown was born in Lafayette, Louisiana, on December 12, 1912, and was a resident of Galveston for thirty-seven years. After Brown assumed ownership of the Welcome Inn, he changed the name of the business to True Friend Grill. Brown operated his grill from that location until 1969, when he moved the business to 2717 Market Street and transitioned the establishment from restaurant to bar. Brown continued to operate the business until his death in 1981. He was survived by his wife, Marjorie, and was buried at Lakeview Cemetery in Galveston.

BUSY BEE GRILL

During the early 1950s, Charles F. Langham owned and operated the Busy Bee Grill at 2619 Market Street. Langham was also a very successful Galveston businessman who operated the Tremont Cleaners and the Busy Bee Taxi Service. Langham was born in Hutto, Texas, on April 27, 1896. He graduated from Hutto High School and Prairie View A&M College. Langham was also a member of Avenue L Baptist Church and a veteran of World War I. He passed away on August 2, 1979, after a lengthy illness. He was interred at Lakeview Cemetery in Galveston. He was survived by his wife, Mary Belle Langham, a brother and two sisters.

MARY JO'S RESTAURANT / CURLY'S CORNER

Mary Jo (Pierce) Caldwell opened Mary Jo's Restaurant at 2804 Church Street in the 1950s and operated the restaurant until 1963. Pink Norwood purchased the location in 1963 and changed the name to Curly's Place Restaurant. Eventually known as Curly's Corner, the business was operated by Norwood until he closed it in 1969. Norwood was born on August 25, 1922, in Arseola, Mississippi. He passed away on November 24, 1999, at UTMB in Galveston. In addition to being a business owner, Norwood was a member of the National Maritime Union. His service was held at Holy Rosary Church followed by burial at Lakeview Cemetery in Galveston. His obituary noted that he was survived by his wife, Margie, granddaughter Lisa Norwood and multiple other relatives.

THREE CEDAR TREES INN RESTAURANT

The Three Cedar Trees Inn Restaurant opened for a few short years in the early 1950s. The restaurant was located at 611 Thirty-Fourth Street and managed by Margaret Shorten. Shorten was born on May 13, 1908, in Jeanerette, Louisiana, and died in Galveston on July 26, 1961. She was an active member of West Point Baptist Church. She is buried at Galveston's Memorial Cemetery.

THREE-TWENTY-NINE DINING ROOM

For a few years during the early 1950s, Claude Stanford operated the Three-Twenty-Nine Dining Room, located at 2823 Market Street. Stanford was born in Matagorda County, Texas, on November 11, 1911. He came to Galveston during the 1930s and was an active citizen of the community. He attended West Point Baptist Church and was involved with ILA Local 329, the local chapter of the NAACP and Boy Scouts Troop 179. He died in Galveston on November 23, 1968, and was interred at Shiloh Missionary Baptist Church Cemetery in Cedar Lane.

4311 POSTOFFICE STREET

Edna Lacy and Johnny D. Ford operated the Roadhouse Café for a short period in the middle of the 1950s. After they closed their cafe in 1957, Freddie Davis took over the location. Davis changed the name to Forty-Third Street Café. By 1958, the location was noted as Dunn's Paradise Inn Restaurant, owned by Recy Dunn Sr., who remained in business through 1961. At the same time, Dunn also owned and operated a

Mobil Gas station at Thirty-First Street and Broadway Boulevard. Dunn was born on June 18, 1926, in Hilly, Louisiana. He passed away at his residence in Deback, Louisiana, on June 14, 2004. He was survived by his wife of fifty-six years, Myrine Foston, six sons, two daughters, twenty-five grandchildren and ten great-grandchildren. His son Recy Dunn Jr. worked to help save Galveston's African American Rosewood Cemetery. The cemetery was established in 1911 and was donated to Galveston Historical Foundation in 2006.

IRENE'S HAMBURGERS & CONEY ISLANDS

In the early 1950s, George McDaniel opened a business at 1314 Twenty-Ninth Street named Irene's Hamburgers & Coney Islands, but the business lasted just a few short years. By 1953, the Galveston City Directory noted that Wilbur Henderson owned and operated the L&M Café at the address. Henderson moved the café in 1958, to 1114 Twenty-Ninth Street, to be closer to the heavily trafficked Broadway Boulevard. Henderson was born in Georgia in 1885. He passed away on November 22, 1978, at UTMB in Galveston. He was a citizen of Galveston for fifty-one years and a veteran of World War I. Henderson was buried at Owensville Cemetery in Franklin, Texas.

RUDY'S SANDWICH SHOP / RUDY'S LUNCH ROOM

Shortly after the City Café closed in 1952, Rudolph R. Wiley opened Rudy's Sandwich Shop at the same location. Wiley also operated Rudy's Lunch Room, located next door at 512 Twenty-Eighth Street.

LITTLE OAK CAFÉ

The Little Oak Café was located at 3814 Ball Street. Frank Irving Sr. owned and operated the café during the early 1950s. After the restaurant's brief existence, Irving operated an unrelated business at the same location for a short time. By 1955, the city directory noted that the building was vacant. Irving was born in Leonville, Louisiana, on March 20, 1903. He came to Galveston in the 1940s and worked as a longshoreman. Irving was a member of the International Longshoremen's Association Local 851 and Mount Pilgrim Baptist Church. He passed away in Houston on November 20, 1992, and was interred at Calvary Catholic Cemetery in Galveston. Among his survivors were son Frank Irving Jr., grandson Frank Irving III and great-grandson Frank Irving IV, all of Oakland, California.

KING'S INN RESTAURANT

In 1956, Phillip Johnson opened the King's Inn Restaurant at 406 Twenty-Sixth Street. The restaurant served the citizens for over twenty years before it closed in 1978. Known as "King," Johnson was born in Orange, Texas, on July 13, 1914. He passed away in Galveston on April 6, 1976. He was interred at Mainland Memorial Cemetery in Hitchcock, Texas. He was a resident of Galveston for over fifty-four years.

ALLEAN'S LUNCH ROOM / CREOLE GRILL & BAR

Allean Stevens opened Allean's Lunch Room in late 1956 at 508 Twenty-Sixth Street and operated it continuously until 1960. After the lunchroom closed, Annie Chatman took over the location and opened the Creole Grill & Bar. In 1964, she closed the business. Chatman was born on August 8, 1904, in Lafayette, Louisiana. A Galveston resident for twenty-five years, she passed away in Hitchcock, Texas, on August 8, 1972, and was interred at Memorial Cemetery in Galveston. She was survived by a brother and a sister.

The Creole Grill & Bar, at Twenty-Sixth and Postoffice Streets. Date unknown. *University of North Texas Libraries, the Portal to Texas History, Texas Historical Commission.*

THE GATEWAY CAFÉ

The Gateway Café opened in the early 1960s at 2728 Winnie Street. Mack Dugan was the proprietor for the few years it was open. During the late 1950s, Dugan operated Mac's Grill at 2619 Market Street.

ETHEL'S LUNCH ROOM

Ethel Harris opened Ethel's Lunch Room at 2810 Ball Street in the early 1960s. The café closed after she died in July 1964. Harris was a resident of Galveston for forty-two years and a member of Mount Calvary Baptist Church. She was survived by a brother, uncle and four aunts. She is buried at Paradise Cemetery in Houston.

OWL CAFÉ

Between 1963 and 1965, John V. Onick owned and operated the Owl Café, located at 2704 Postoffice Street. Onick was born on April 7, 1908, in Marshall, Texas. He passed away on May 24, 1970, in Galveston. He is buried at Rising Star Cemetery in La Marque.

Chapter 6

Recipes

Authors' Picks

GLADYS BERNICE CAMPBELL

"Mrs. Campbell," as she was known by many Galveston Independent School District students and faculty, was the cafeteria manager for Booker T. Washington Elementary School and later George W. Carver Elementary School. When George W. Carver and Goliad Elementary Schools combined in 1975 to form the present L.A. Morgan Elementary School, she became the new cafeteria manager. She retired after thirty-eight years of service in the GISD kitchens.

Gladys Bernice Campbell. *Courtesy Alice Gatson.*

"Bernice," as she was known by family, grew up in Live Oak and Sealy, Texas, where her parents worked the fields. She started cooking at an early age and became the primary cook for a family of five—herself plus her parents and two siblings. Bernice was the oldest of the three siblings and enjoyed cooking. Her culinary talents and love for cooking were passed down to her three grandsons and one granddaughter, who were always on the phone asking, "Grandma, how do you cook this?" Bernice always replied, "Get some paper and write this down so you can have this next time you need it." Their favorite things to try to make were her seafood gumbo and potato salad. Each grandchild has their favorite recipe from "Grandma," and each "Grand," as she called them, shared them in her honor.

Angel Biscuits
Shared by Rosalyn Gatson

5 cups flour
1 cups shortening
½ cup sugar
1 package dry yeast
3 teaspoons baking powder
2 tablespoons warm water
1 teaspoon soda
2 cups buttermilk
1 teaspoon salt

Sift dry ingredients together; cut in shortening. Dissolve yeast in warm water and add with buttermilk to dry mixture. Mix well and turn out on lightly floured board. Add more flour if necessary. Roll to ¼-inch thickness. Cut, then dip in melted butter. Bake at 400 degrees for 15 minutes or until golden brown.

Shrimp Étouffée
Shared by Adrian Crooks

¼ cup cooking oil
1 ½ pounds raw shrimp, cleaned
½ cup flour
½ bell pepper, chopped
1 onion, chopped
5 sprigs parsley, chopped
½ cup green onions, chopped
1 large tomato, chopped
2 cloves garlic, chopped
2 ribs celery, chopped
Salt and pepper

In a pot, make a roux with oil and flour, cook to light brown. Add remaining ingredients to pot and cover. Cook on low heat for about 30 minutes or when shrimp are done and a nice gravy is present. Stir, and cook slow and on low heat. Serve with rice.

Peanut Butter Cookies
Shared by Christopher Gatson

3½ cups flour
½ cup milk
¾ teaspoon baking soda
1 cup butter or margarine
½ teaspoon salt
1½ cups peanut butter
1½ cups sugar
3 large eggs
½ cup brown sugar (packed)
1 tablespoon vanilla

Combine dry ingredients. Blend butter, peanut butter, sugars, eggs and vanilla on medium speed. Add to dry ingredients, blend on low speed, then medium speed. Drop on cookie sheet and flatten with fork. Bake at 350 degrees for 12–15 minutes or until lightly brown.

Red Beans and Rice
Shared by Gary Crooks Jr.

1 pound dry kidney beans
½ teaspoon cayenne pepper
¼ cup olive oil
1 teaspoon Cajun seasoning
1 large onion, chopped
1 pound Andouille sausage, sliced
1 green bell pepper, chopped
2 stalks celery, chopped
2 tablespoons minced garlic

6 cups water
2 bay leaves

Rinse beans and soak in large pot overnight. In skillet, heat olive oil over medium heat and add onion, bell pepper, garlic and celery. Cook for about 3 minutes. Rinse beans and put in large pot with 6 cups of water, stir cooked vegetables and sliced sausage into beans. Season with bay leaves, cayenne pepper and Cajun seasoning. Bring to a boil and turn fire down and cook for 2½ hours. Serve over steamed white rice.

LILLIE RHODES DAVIS

Lillie Rhodes Davis. *Courtesy Tommie Boudreaux.*

Lillie Rhodes was born in Mexia, Texas, on December 12, 1919, the oldest and only girl of the five children born to Ezekiel and Mary Rhodes. Lillie married Tom Davis of Brenham, Texas, in 1939, and the couple moved to Galveston the same year.

Lillie was introduced to the kitchen at an early age. She was taught to cook by her mother and grandmother without using measuring cups or measuring spoons. When preparing a dish, the readiness of a dish was judged by sight and taste. She taught her three children, Mary, Tommie and James, to cook the same way. However, when her four grandsons, Mark and Trent Boudreaux and James and Tommie Crayton, became interested in preparing her dishes, she purchased measuring cups, spoons and other kitchen gadgets and measured as she prepared a dish and wrote the recipes down and gave them the recipes. Lillie passed away on October 24, 2013, but her beloved recipes live on. Here are a few favorites from a book of recipes she gave to her grandson Trent David Boudreaux as a wedding gift.

Fried Cabbage

Use salt pork. Cut in thin strips. Fry slowly until oil is out. Wash cabbage. Chop in small pieces. (Do not add water). Add cabbage and one jalapeño pepper, toss and cover tight until cabbage is limp. Stir and cook until water is gone.

Squash Casserole

About 3 pounds squash
1 large onion, chopped
2 eggs
1 teaspoon salt
3 tablespoons sugar
1 teaspoon black pepper
½ pound Jimmy Dean Pork Sausage
1 tablespoon flaked onions
1 cup bread crumbs
1 stick butter

Wash squash. Cut into pieces. Place ¾ butter on bottom of pot. Add chopped onions. Place squash on top of onions. Add squash, salt, sugar and black pepper. (Do not add water.) Steam on low flame with lid tightly on for about 10 minutes. Stir occasionally. Cook until tender, drain excess water off. Mash well. Add flake onion, bread crumbs, except 3 tablespoons. Sauté pork sausage, stirring and crumbling with a fork about 10 or 15 minutes. Add to mixture. Add beaten eggs. Mix well. Sprinkle bread crumbs over casserole. Dot pieces of butter over casserole. Preheat oven to 325 degrees. Bake about 45 minutes.

Sweet Potato Pie

Gather 2 slightly round sweet potatoes large enough to make 3 cups of cooked potatoes. Boil potatoes with skin on until done. Cover in cold water. Pull skin off, leaving warm enough for your butter to melt. Mash and set aside. Make pie crust:

3 cups flour
¾ cup Crisco shortening
1 teaspoon salt
¼ cup cold water

Push flour to one side of mixing bowl. On empty side, add Crisco and salt. With a fork gradually mix flour with Crisco with about half of the flour until crumbled fine. Gradually work in water to make a stiff ball. Roll out and place in pie pan. Be sure to spread over edge.

For the pie filling:

3 cups potatoes, cooked and mashed
1 ½ cups sugar, or to taste
½ teaspoon salt
½ teaspoon cinnamon
½ teaspoon nutmeg
1 teaspoon vanilla
¾ stick of butter
2 eggs
½ cup can milk
½ teaspoon all spice

Add all flavors, sugar, butter and potatoes together in mixing bowl. Beat with mixer. Add egg yolks and milk. Beat well. In a separate bowl, beat whites of eggs. Fold in and stir well. Pour in pie pan. Back in oven at 350 degrees for about 45 minutes to 1 hour.

Grilled Chicken Creole

2 pounds chicken breasts
1 cup Louisiana brand hot sauce
2 tablespoons butter or oleo
2 tablespoons onion flakes
2 large cloves of garlic
¼ cup chopped bell pepper
½ cup chopped celery
1 tablespoon cornstarch
¼ cup tomato juice (from the can of tomatoes)
1 ½ teaspoon sugar
1 teaspoon Tony Chachere's seasoning
1 teaspoon dry parsley flakes
Dash of black pepper
1 large can (48 ounces) chopped tomatoes

Poke holes in chicken using a fork and place in a gallon-size Ziploc bag with hot sauce. Marinate chicken 4–8 hours.

Melt butter in a heavy pot, add onion flakes, garlic, bell pepper, celery and parsley. Cook, stirring until tender. In a separate bowl, combine cornstarch with tomato juice. Add sugar, Tony Chachere's and chopped tomatoes to the cooked mixture and continue stirring. Add cornstarch mixture, stir and cook until slightly thickened. Cover and remove from heat.

Remove chicken breasts from the bag and pat dry using a paper towel. Preheat a charcoal or gas grill to 500 degrees. Grill chicken breast for 3–5 minutes per side or until internal temperature is 165 degrees. Slice chicken into bite-size pieces.

Serve grilled chicken with sauce over rice.

VIOLA SCULL FEDFORD AND FLORENCE HENDERSON

The recipes for baked crab and for shrimp cocktail were handed down to the family members of Viola Scull Fedford. She may have learned to cook the delectable baked crab dish from her own mother, Mrs. Florence Scull (born in 1867), as she was the only girl in her household. Viola Scull Fedford obtained her crabmeat by catching crabs early in the morning from knee-deep water in the Gulf of Mexico and often took her Henderson grandchildren along on these "crabbing" trips, which were always followed by a baked crab dinner.

The shrimp cocktail recipe presented here was that of her daughter Florence Henderson. It was the first course of every Thanksgiving dinner. Florence cooked the Thanksgiving dinner with the help of her mother, Viola, and every year, the family recalls how much they looked forward to the shrimp cocktail.

Florence Scull (*right*) and Florence Fedford Henderson (*on steps*). *Courtesy of Diane Henderson.*

Baked Crabs

1 pound crabmeat (mixed or claw meat preferred)
4 slices bread (day-old is fine)
1 small onion, diced
1 stalk of celery, diced
1 small bell pepper, diced
1 egg
3 tablespoons margarine
Dash of salt and pepper
Crab shells (back)

If using crab shells, cleanse thoroughly. Soak in baking soda solution; rinse well and dry. Note: Glass shells or a glass baking dish or 9-inch glass pie dish may be used instead of natural shells.

Set aside 2 slices of the bread for topping. Place them in the oven with a low temperature until crisp enough to roll into crumbs using a rolling pin. (If you prefer, ready-to-use bread crumbs can be bought.)

Sauté the onion, celery and bell pepper in margarine until tender. The onion should be golden or tan in color. Meanwhile, put the remaining bread in a mixing bowl and wet completely. Squeeze out excess water. Mix soggy bread with the crabmeat, sautéed vegetables and egg. Season to taste and fill shells (or glass dish) with the mixture. Cover (top) the mixture with bread crumbs and bake at 400 degrees for about 10 minutes. Serve warm.

Shrimp Cocktail

1–2 pounds shrimp
1–2 boiled eggs
8 ounces tomato catsup
1–2 ounces Worcestershire Sauce
*1 teaspoon grated onion**
1 teaspoon salad mustard

4–5 drops Tabasco
Dash of garlic powder or garlic salt

Shell and de-vein shrimp. Put in saucepan with water just enough to cover shrimp. Bring to a boil and simmer 4–5 minutes. Do not overcook. Shrimp are done when they turn red. Drain immediately and allow to cool. Place shrimp in cocktail cups and top with minced boiled egg. (If using other than small cocktail shrimp, cut into pieces.)

Mix remaining ingredients to make sauce and pour over shrimp. Serve with crackers.

*Onion powder, salt or juice may be used according to preference

RECIPES OF REEDY CHAPEL AFRICAN METHODIST EPISCOPAL CHURCH, FOUNDED 1848

In 1848, the parishioners and trustees of Galveston's Methodist Episcopal Church South decided to establish a church for their slaves under the Methodist Episcopal bishop. On March 18 of that year, the trustees purchased property at Broadway and Twentieth Street for this purpose, and later that year, a church building and parsonage were erected and given to the slaves as the "Negro Methodist Episcopal Church South." In 1866, the church was reorganized as the first African Methodist Episcopal Church in Texas by the Reverend M.M. Clark. It was turned over to its Black membership by the Methodist Episcopal trustees on March 13, 1867, and renamed Reedy Chapel after the Reverend Houston Reedy, second pastor of the church.

In 1885, a fire that destroyed forty square blocks of Galveston burned the 1848 church. A year later, the present Reedy Chapel AME Church was built. The contractor was E.F. Campbell, and the renowned Norris Wright Cuney, a Reedy parishioner, laid the masonry. The building, designed by architect Benjamin G. Chisolm, combines Gothic Revival architecture with regional craftsmanship and is distinguished by the pyramid-roofed tower rising out of its body. The steeply pitched roof consists of a heavy timber

The historic Reedy Chapel, founded in 1848.

scissor truss framing system. The sanctuary still uses the eighteen-foot-tall Gothic pipe organ, built of ash with carved walnut trim in 1872 by E. and G.G. and Hastings of New York. The organ was donated to Reedy Chapel by the Trinity Episcopal Church of Galveston.

Reedy Chapel has welcomed thirty-eight pastors in its more than one hundred years. The first two annual conferences of the African Methodist Episcopal Church to be held in Texas were hosted by Reedy. The first, convened by Bishop Jabez P. Campbell in 1867, was presided over by his representative, Reverend T.W. Stringer. The following year, Bishop James A. Shorter led the second annual conference, the first Texas meeting of Methodist men of color to be conducted by and for African Americans.

Reedy Chapel AME Church was placed in the National Register of Historic Places in 1984. The dumpling recipe is from a collection of church recipes published in 1987 by Bernice Gardner.

Annie's Dumplings

2 cups flour
½ cup Crisco
½ teaspoon salt
1 teaspoon baking powder
1 beaten egg
½ cup + 1 tablespoon milk

Cut Crisco into flour, salt and baking powder. Blend egg with milk and stir into dry mixture. Turn dough out on well-floured board, roll to ⅛ inch thickness and cut in 2-by-4-inch strips.

Dumplings may be used with berries for berries and dumplings or drop into hot chicken broth for chicken and dumplings.

For berries and dumplings:
Mix 1 pound fresh or frozen berries with 4 tablespoons sugar, ¼ cup water and 1 tablespoon lemon juice. Cook over medium heat until fruit releases its juices and bubbles. Drop dumplings into fruit, lower heat and cook 15–20 minutes.

LEE STRAMBLER HOLMES

Lee Strambler was born in La Grange, Texas, on June 8, 1938, and was one of seven children born to James and Connie Strambler. In March 1957, Lee married Wilbert Holmes in La Grange; to their union, six children were born: Victor, Shirley, Wilma, Dwayne, Stephen and Stanley. The Holmes family moved to Galveston County in 1966 and established their home in the community of Dickinson.

When Lee was just twelve years old, her mother began to teach her how to cook. Lessons weren't always navigated using written recipes and were often led simply by way of verbal instruction. Lee, in turn, taught her children to cook many of her own dishes using the same technique. Her fried chicken, known lovingly as "Mama's Fried Chicken," is still a family favorite.

Lee once said: "I enjoyed cooking for my family. Each meal I cooked was made with love. I always wanted to make sure of two things when cooking—that there would be enough food for everyone and that my food would be tasty." She always succeeded at both.

Mama's Fried Chicken

Before you begin, gather: 1 whole chicken (cut), large bowl, two large pans, brown paper bag or large plastic bag, oil, cast-iron deep skillet and all-purpose flour.

1 cup buttermilk
2 tablespoons paprika
2 teaspoons pepper
1 teaspoon garlic powder
½ teaspoon onion powder
1 ½ teaspoons salt
¼ teaspoon ground sage

Mix the above ingredients together with the buttermilk. Place pieces of chicken in a large pan and pour buttermilk mixture over chicken. Baste each piece and allow it to marinate 1–2 hours.

After chicken has marinated, pour 2 cups of flour into the bag (paper/plastic). Put 2–3 pieces of chicken at a time into the bag and shake vigorously until the chicken is fully covered in the flour. Take chicken out of the bag and place in a large pan. Repeat until each piece of chicken has been coated with flour. Allow the pieces of chicken to rest in the pan for 10–15 minutes so the flour can cleave to the chicken.

Make sure your grease is hot, then place chicken parts into the grease and cook on each side for 8–10 minutes, turning side to side (larger pieces can take longer) until chicken is golden brown (done). Remove from skillet and drain on paper towels before serving.

About Galveston Historical Foundation

Galveston Historical Foundation (GHF) was formed as the Historical Society of Galveston in 1871 and merged with a new organization formed in 1954 as a nonprofit entity devoted to historic preservation and history in Galveston County. Over the last sixty years, GHF has expanded its mission to encompass community redevelopment, historic preservation advocacy, maritime preservation, coastal resiliency and stewardship of historic properties. GHF embraces a broader vision of history and architecture that encompasses advancements in environmental and natural sciences and their intersection with historic buildings and coastal life and conceives of history as an engaging story of individual lives and experiences on Galveston Island from the nineteenth century to the present day.

#GALVESTON HISTORY

About the Contributors

Gregory Samford grew up in Galveston and graduated from Ball High School in 1975. After he received a bachelor's degree and a master's degree from Stephen F. Austin State University in Nacogdoches, Texas, he returned to the island, where he worked for the University of Texas Medical Branch. Recently retired, Greg is a congregation member of the historic Arcadia First Baptist Church located in Santa Fe, Texas.

Tommie D. Boudreaux is a retired Galveston independent school administrator who graduated from the historic Central High School, the first high school for African Americans in Texas. She has served as the chair of the Galveston Historical Foundation's African American Heritage Committee and is the coauthor of *African Americans of Galveston*.

Ella Lewis is a native Galvestonian and graduate of the historic Central High School. With degrees from HBCU Prairie View A&M University and the University of Houston Clear Lake (UHCL), her life's work has centered on education through her service as a teacher, an administrator and an adjunct professor at UHCL. Ella is an avid reader who enjoys writing poetry, serving on boards that serve the Galveston community and working as a volunteer in areas where needed. She resides in Galveston, where she works with children through the organization Communities in Schools.

Alice M. Gatson is a retired biomedical technologist. Born on the island, she graduated from the historic Central High School, served as a chair of Galveston Historical Foundation's African American Heritage Committee and coauthored *African Americans of Galveston* with Tommie Boudreaux.